ABERYSTWYTH HARBOUR

ABERYSTWYTH HARBOUR

AN ILLUSTRATED HISTORY

BY
WILLIAM TROUGHTON

THE NATIONAL LIBRARY OF WALES
ABERYSTWYTH
1997

ISBN 0 - 907158 - 98 - 6

Designed by: Enfys Jenkins.

Produced and Printed by:
David Eldridge, Alan Thomas & Michael Binks,
members of the Printing Department,
The National Library of Wales, Aberystwyth.

Contents

Fishing boats in the Gap 1954.   (Photo Album 706 PG 221/101)

INTRODUCTION

The National Library of Wales is one of the United Kingdom's premier reference libraries and is renowned as a storehouse of the nation's treasures. It houses some four million books and periodicals, forty thousand manuscripts, four and a half thousand framed works of art, nearly two million maps and half a million photographs.

Much material of Aberystwyth interest that would normally have been expected to find its way to a local museum found its way to the National Library of Wales as there was then no museum in the town. The Department of Pictures and Maps is therefore blessed with a treasure trove of material relating to Aberystwyth. Items range from the earliest view of the harbour by J C Ibbetson who visited in 1792, through topographical prints from the early nineteenth century, the work of the Welsh primitive (an unknown artist who flourished ca. 1840) to the work of pier-head artists who painted Aberystwyth vessels when they entered far away ports. Bought by the ship's captain and carefully stowed in his cabin

until hung on the wall in his front room these paintings are vivid and colourful records of the days of sail.

With the advent of photography came grittier images of a working port, most the work of photographers whose identities have since been surrendered to the mists of time. The first half of the twentieth century has been ably documented by Arthur Lewis

Arthur Lewis, known as *Lewis the Mart* took many of the photographs in this book. Without the Arthur Lewis Collection it is doubtful if this book could have been compiled. Born and brought up in Aberystwyth Arthur Lewis inherited his love of both ships and photography from his father. Both Arthur Lewis's grandfathers had been sea captains and his father had been a ship's carpenter before settling down and opening a small photographic studio in Great Darkgate Street. Arthur Lewis too had gone to sea, but after a bout of ill-health had returned to Aberystwyth. The family later bought larger premises in Great Darkgate Street which they called The Mart where they

sold a wide variety of household items. The photographic studio was in the back. Arthur Lewis enjoyed documenting the arrival and departure of vessels in the harbour. This was no mean feat, often involving poor lighting conditions and long periods spent waiting for vessels to arrive. The great variety of vantage points used is a tribute to his patience and enthusiasm.

Another photographer of note was John Challinor, at one time senior lecturer in Geology at the University College of Wales, Aberystwyth. He too turned his attention to the harbour with success.

Barely alluded to in this book but of considerable importance to scholars of the town's maritime history are the crew agreements for nearly six hundred Aberystwyth registered vessels to be found in the Department of Manuscripts and Records. These date from 1863-1913 and provide details of the crew, their conditions and an indication of the voyages undertaken.

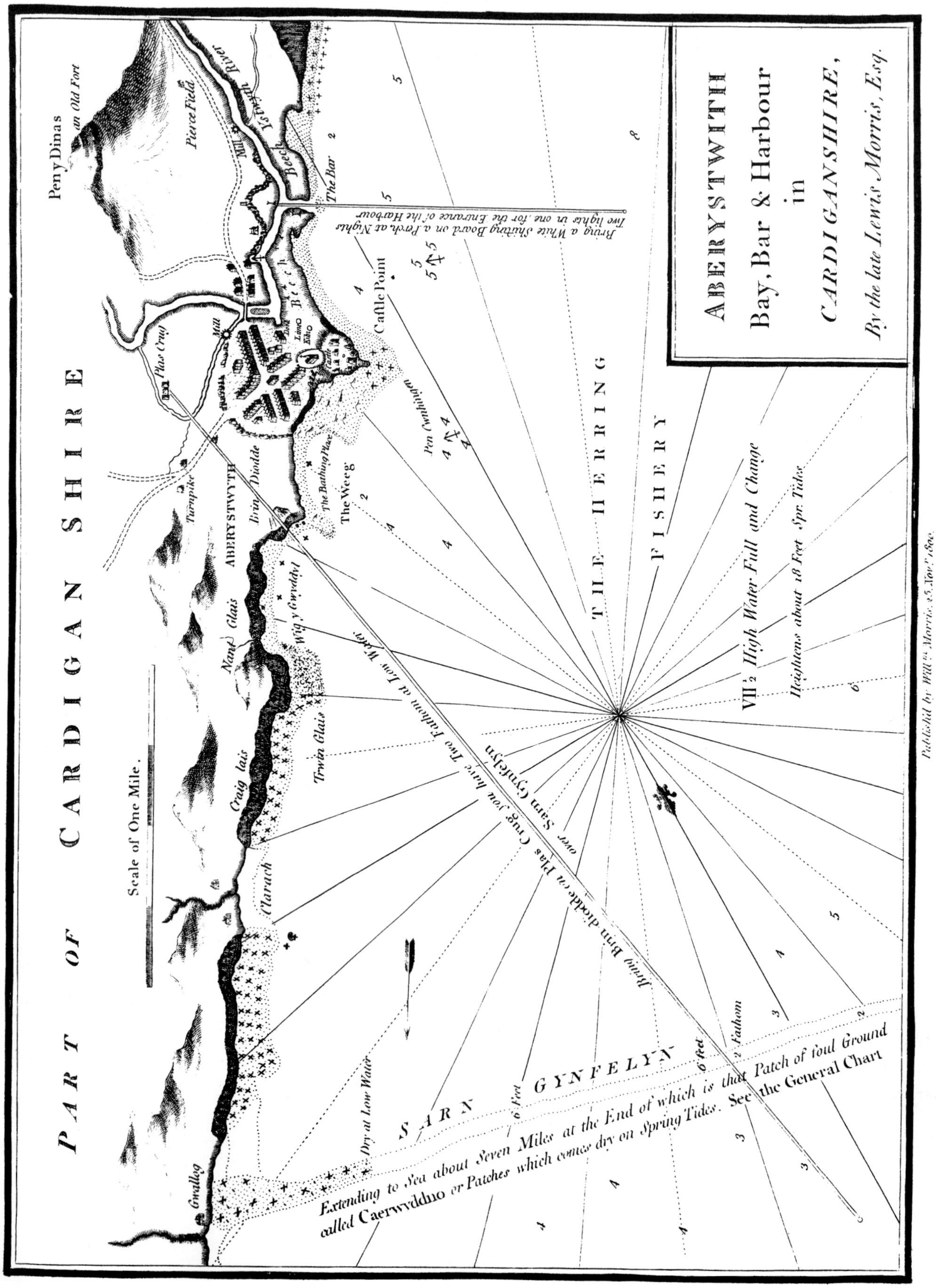

ABERYSTWYTH
Bay, Bar & Harbour
in
CARDIGANSHIRE,
By the late Lewis Morris, Esq.

(NLW Printed Maps)

Lewis Morris's map of Aberystwyth, published in 1809.

EARLY DEVELOPMENT

The source of the earliest complete study of Aberystwyth Harbour comes from Lewis Morris. Commissioned by the Admiralty to survey the coast of Wales in 1737, it was not until 1748 that he reached Aberystwyth. What he found did not impress him greatly, though he was quick to see the potential of the harbour and stated that that the town was one of the great fisheries of Wales with fifty nine small sloops operating out of the harbour during the herring season. He was of the opinion that the harbour could be improved by excavating an entrance for the River Rheidol near the castle. Later he suggested building a stone pier from what is now the bottom of Pier Street out to sea along the wave cut platform to provide a sheltered anchorage. This was later tried but proved a disaster.

Until 1762 the harbour at Aberystwyth came under the jurisdiction of Aberdyfi and had only a fleet of fishing boats which carried cargoes such as bark, lead ore and timber in the coasting trade outside the fishing season. In addition some lead ore was exported by larger Dutch vessels which sometimes had problems in leaving the harbour. The most important imports were limestone for use as fertiliser and salt used in preserving herring. In the hinterland beyond Aberystwyth the lead mines had become increasingly active. Those involved in exporting lead ore found the necessity of consulting with the Aberdyfi customs office increasingly frustrating and petitioned Parliament to move the customs house to Aberystwyth. This was achieved in 1763 and helped boost lead mining and in turn the town and harbour. The increased trade also focussed attention on the need to improve the harbour to enable larger vessels to arrive and depart with greater convenience. To this end an Act of Parliament was secured in 1780 to allow improvements to be made. Trustees were appointed to oversee the running of the harbour and met monthly in local taverns. Although able to borrow money against the security of the harbour dues the trustees chose not to spend anything other than the absolute minimum on repairs and minor improvements even though the number and size of ships registered at Aberystwyth was steadily increasing. In 1792 there were 99 vessels registered at the port with an average size of 36 tons. Exports outstripped imports at the time. From the district went lead ore, slates, charcoal, oak poles and occasional cargoes of pig Iron. Imports were of a more general nature and included sugar, molasses, whale oil, tobacco, wine and spirits, cheese, salt, earthenware goods, wearing apparel and rye. More unusual one off items included painters' colours, frying pans and bundles of paper.

By 1815 the number of vessels registered increased with an average size of 57 tons. Combined with an increase in shipbuilding activity and later the advent of regular coasting services to London, Liverpool and Bristol, the trustees were forced to contemplate drastic action. To this end they hired a Mr Nimmo, an engineer to advise on proposed improvements. His plan met with satisfaction and George Bush was engaged to put the scheme into practice. Work on the stone pier commenced in 1836, the same year that another Act of Parliament was secured to enable more money to be borrowed. Stone was quarried from Alltwen on the south side of Tan-y-bwlch beach and transported along a specially constructed tramway to the new pier. Construction of a wharf, quay wall and warehouses on the interior of Ro-fawr and the 260 yard pier took years to achieve. In addition the seaward side of Ro-fawr was stabilised by erecting groins intended to guide and form the beach to the proper slope required for resisting the force of the sea. In addition the level of Ro-fawr was raised ten feet to stop the sea washing over it. The southern end of Ro-fawr was further protected from erosion by large blocks of stone anchored with wooden piles.

The harbour entrance at low tide by J C Ibbetson, 1792.

(Framed works, PE4090)

The harbour c1840. Ro-fawr has been stabilised with wooden stakes to prevent it from being washed away. (Cardiganshire Topographical Prints, PB5139)

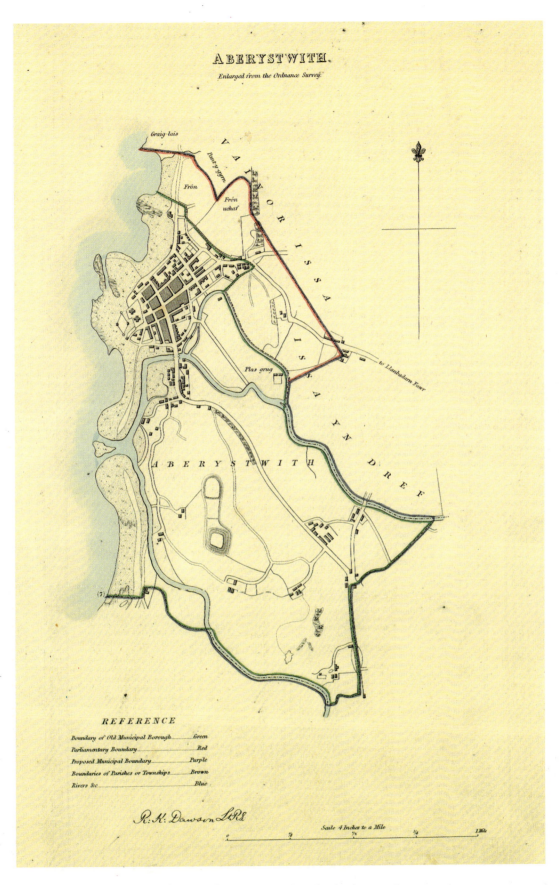

The town of Aberystwyth c1835. Note the sandbar at the harbour entrance.
(Cardiganshire Printed Maps, M1293)

PORT & HARBOUR OF ABERYSTWYTH.

A Table of the Rates and Duties to be collected within the said Port and Harbour, in pursuance of an Act of the 20th GEO. III. chap. 26.

INWARDS.

For every ship or Vessel from Ireland, Isle of Man, or any part of Great Britain, per Ton of the Tonnage thereof, One Penny.

From any other Place, Three-Half-Pence per Ton (except His Majesty's Ships or Vessels of War, or any Ship or Vessel employed in Fishing only).

	s.	d.			s.	d.	
Ale	0	6	per Barrel	Iron (Pig)	0	1	per Ton
Brandy	2	0	per Ton	Iron Stone	0	1	per Ton
Butter	1	6	per Ton	Lime Stone	0	1	per Ton
Brick	0	2	per Ton	Lead	1	0	per Ton
Brick Tiles	0	2	per Ton	Logwood	1	0	per Ton
Battery	2	6	per Ton	Linen Cloth	0	2	per Piece
Balk	0	6	per Ton	Lamb and Kid Skins	0	6	per Hundred
Boards of all sorts	1	0	per Hundred	Molasses	0	6	per Hogshead
Cheese	1	6	per Ton	Malt	0	3	per Quarter
Coal	0	2	per Ton	Malt Liquors	1	0	pr. barrel [50lb.
Culm	0	2	per Ton	Millinery	0	6	per box or truss of
Cloth (Linen)	0	2	per Piece	Oak Timber	0	6	per Ton
Cloth (Narrow Woollen)	0	3	per Piece	Oak Boards	1	0	per Hundred
Cloth (Broad Woollen)	1	0	per Piece	Oil	1	0	per Last
Calf Skins	0	6	per Hundred	Pitch	1	0	per Last
Cider	1	0	per Hogshead	Pig Iron	0	1	per Ton
Candles	2	6	per Ton	Pulse	0	3	per Quarter
Clover Seeds	2	6	per Ton	Paper	0	1	per Bale
Corn	0	3	per Quarter	Porter	0	6	per Barrel
Deal Boards	1	0	per Hundred	Rum	2	0	per Ton
Earthen Ware (British)	0	2	per Crate	Rice	1	0	per Ton
Earthen Ware (Foreign)	1	0	per Crate	Raft or Timber	0	6	per Ton
Flax	1	6	per Ton	Salt	0	6	per Ton
Foreign Spirits	2	0	per Ton	Sheep Skins	0	6	per Hundred
Goat Skins	0	6	per Hundred	Sugar	0	6	per Hogshead
Grass Seeds	2	6	per Ton	Soap	2	6	per Ton
Grain of all sorts	0	3	per Quarter	Slates	0	2	per Ton
Gun Powder	0	6	per Cwt	Spirituous Liquors	2	0	per Ton
Hemp	1	6	per Ton	Treacle	0	6	per Hogshead
Herrings	0	1	per Barrel	Tobacco	2	0	per Hogshead
Hides	2	6	per Hundred	Tar	1	0	per Last
Hops	2	6	per Ton [50lb.	Turnip Seeds	2	6	per Ton
Haberdashery	0	6	per box or truss of	Wine	2	0	per Ton
Iron (Wrought)	1	0	per Ton	Woollen (Broad Cloth)	1	0	per Piece
Iron (Unwrought)	1	0	per Ton	Woollen (Narrow Cloth)	0	3	per Piece

And for all other Goods, Wares, or Merchandise, not before enumerated, the Sum of One Penny in or out of every Twenty Shillings of the Value thereof; and Payment shall be made in proportion for any greater or lesser Weight, Quantity, or Number of any Goods, Wares, or Merchandise, chargeable to the said Duties, so that such Rate or Duty shall in no case be less than One Penny.

RATES AND DUTIES OUTWARDS.

	s.	d.			s.	d.	
Bark	0	3	per Ton	Herrings	0	1	per Barrel
Black Jack	0	2	per Ton	Lead	1	0	per Ton
Butter	1	6	per Ton	Malt Liquor	0	6	per Barrel
Cheese	1	6	per Ton	Ore	0	6	per Ton
Corn, Malt, and Pulse	0	1	per Quarter	Slates	0	2	per Ton

The foregoing Rates and Duties are payable on all Ships or Vessels, Goods, Wares, or Merchandise, that shall be landed or shipped in the said Harbour, or any other Place between Craig Lais and Craig yr Alltwen, being the Limits thereof.

If any Tenant, Lessee, or other Persons, shall demand or collect more than is specified in the foregoing Table, he shall forfeit treble the Sum so demanded or collected, together with all Costs and Charges attending the Prosecution, to be recovered, levied, and applied as the Act directs.

And to the intent that the said Rates or Duties may be duly answered and paid, IT IS ENACTED, That no Collector, Comptroller, Receiver of Entries, Ship Surveyor, Searcher, Waiter, or other Officer of the Customs at Aberystwyth, shall at any time give or make out any Cocket, or other Discharge, or take any Report outwards for any Ship or other Vessel, or permit any Ship or other Vessel to go out of the said Harbour, or any Creek, Shore, or Landing-Place, within the Bounds or Limits aforesaid, until the Master, Owner, or other Person having the Rule or Command of such Ship or other Vessel, shall produce a Certificate under the hand of the Collector of the Rates or Duties that the same has been fully paid, or secured to be paid, under the Penalty of Twenty Pounds, to be recovered by an Action of Debt, Bill, Plaint, or Information, in any of His Majesty's Courts of Record at Westminster.

[PRINTED AND SOLD BY E. WILLIAMS, ABERYSTWYTH.

Charges for the Port & Harbour Of Aberystwyth introduced c1800.   (Posters, PY0587)

An engraving from c1840 showing the newly completed stone pier.   (Cardiganshire Topographical Prints, PZ3285/2)

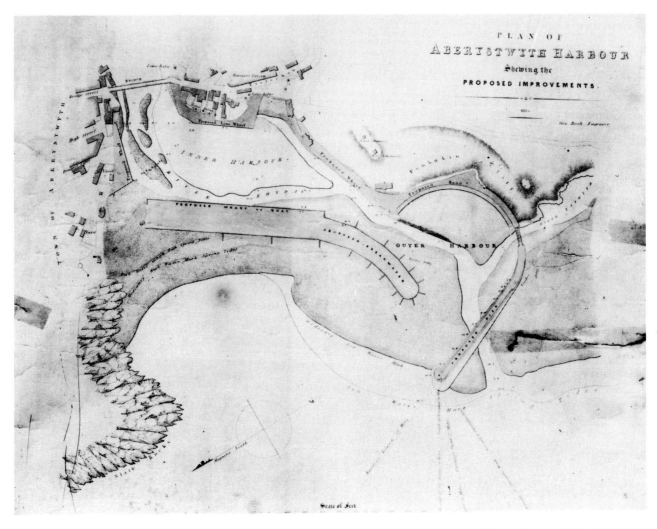

The proposed improvements to the harbour suggested by George Bush in 1834.   (Photo Album 1262, PZ5463/95)

The harbour c1870. Shipbuilding is in progress and baulks of timber visible in Thomas Jones' yard.
(Photo Album 83, P 1022213)

The harbour c1870. A number of fishing smacks can be seen along with an unidentified steamer moored in the lower harbour.
(Photo Album 1266 PZ 5467116)

AN ERA OF PROSPERITY

The works undertaken by George Bush created a deeper channel which had enough force to wash away the bar at the entrance to the harbour. In addition the stone pier prevented the entrance being blocked by checking the effect of longshore drift of material from Tan-y-bwlch beach which also threatened to block the entry of the rivers into the sea. This meant that the harbour could be left or entered readily, depending only on the state of the tide. Traffic increased dramatically and it was not unusual for four or five vessels to enter the harbour on the same day. To aid vessels entering the harbour a capstan was later placed on the stone pier and two buoys were moored some 400 yards off shore as moorings until the tide was suitable for entry into the harbour. A black ball was hoisted halfway up a flagpole on the pier to show when there was 9 feet of water on the bar. Any ship wishing to enter the harbour would signal its intention to the harbourmaster with a light. Hobblers were on hand to help vessels entering the harbour. These were usually retired seamen who attached ropes between the vessel and the capstan on the pier. Turning the capstan enabled vessels to negotiate the right angle turn into the harbour entrance They were paid two shillings for every 20 tons the vessel carried. This was shared equally among the men with the exception of the boat-

owner responsible for taking the ropes to the ship, who received more. The process was repeated when a vessel left the harbour.

In the space of twenty years the harbour dues increased ten-fold, though most of this went on paying interest to those who loaned money to the scheme in the first place. Despite the increase in trade the rapid growth of ports in South Wales meant that Aberystwyth lost its place as the third largest port in Wales as it had been in 1837. Shipbuilding and repairing assumed a greater importance and supported ancillary industries such

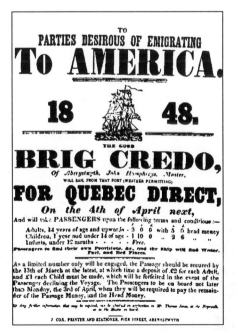

Credo was usually employed importing timber into Aberystwyth but occasionally carried a human cargo.
(Posters XHE 'D')

as rope makers, sail makers, blockmakers, and a chain, cable & anchor works. Shipbuilding and repairing was carried out on the area now known as the gap and on the site of the former sewage works, themselves built in 1925. The majority of locally built ships were owned by local shareholders. Each ship was divided into 64 shares which would be held by local tradesmen, those involved in their construction and perhaps the master and his family. Foremost among Aberystwyth shipowners were Thomas Jones the Ropemaker and his descendants.

The port of Aberystwyth was given a further boost in 1847 when a treasury warrant extended the jurisdiction of the port to include all creeks and havens from New Quay to the north bank of the Dysynni, just north of Tywyn. This included both Aberaeron and New Quay, substantially increasing the number of ships registered at the port. By 1850 213 vessels with a combined tonnage of 12,458 tons were registered here and employed an estimated 900 men. Such was the number of vessels associated with the town that in 1853 the Aberystwyth Mutual Ship Insurance Society was formed. This enabled owners to insure vessels in Aberystwyth instead of London, saving both inconvenience and brokers fees whilst keeping premiums in the town. A similar society was founded in New Quay four years later.

A view of the lower harbour, c1840. When aligned the two towers on Penyrancor guided ships safely into the harbour.   (N.L.W. Drawing Volume 56)

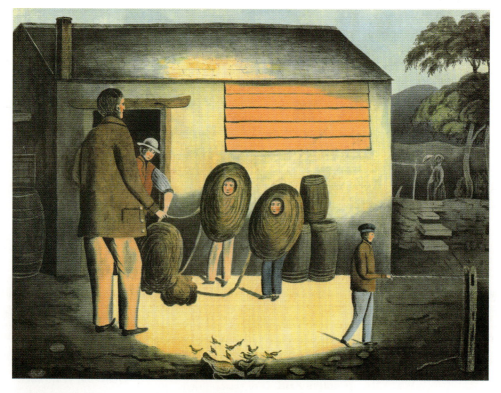

Ropemaking was an industry closely allied to shipbuilding and repairing. There were two ropewalks in the town, one parallel to Queens Road, the other at the eastern end of Dinas Terrace.   (Welsh Primitive, Carmarthen Museum)

IMPORTS & EXPORTS

During this period the most important exports were lead and zinc ores. sent for refining in Llanelli, Bristol and on the River Dee. Much of this was stored in a warehouse behind St David's Wharf. Other significant exports were oak bark, in demand from Irish tanneries and oak poles for use in coal mines as props.

Imports were more varied and included south Wales coal, limestone, various household goods from London, Liverpool and Bristol, roofing slates from north Wales, flagstones from Cardigan and most importantly timber.

Coal and coal dust, known as culm, were imported for a variety of purposes. Culm was cheaper than lump coal and used by the majority of the inhabitants for heating and cooking, coal being the preserve of the gentry and the better off. Amongst the importers of culm were David Roberts who used it in his brewery. He also imported Guinness direct from Dublin. Culm was mixed with limestone in the lime kilns to produce lime for fertilising the fields. The number of lime kilns still to be seen on the Trefechan side of the harbour illustrate the importance of this trade at one time. Lime kilns are still to be seen elsewhere on the coast at convenient landing places such as Wallog, Morfa Bychan and Llanrhystud.

Both the lead mining and ship-building industries relied heavily on regular supplies of timber. This demand could not be met locally and so timber had to be imported. By the middle of the last century timber was being imported

from the Baltic area and from North America, usually in the form of deals or unsawn timber. This timber arrived on Aberystwyth owned vessels. Into this category came the likes of *Credo, Rhydol,* *Eigen, Hope, Wellington, Ivanhoe* and *Crusader.* Usually the outward voyage was made in ballast though during the 1840's there are instances of timber ships carrying emigrants on their outward

(Above & Below) Communication with other ports was maintained by a number of scheduled services as these hand-bills illustrate. The *Speculation,* a 62 ton schooner was built in Aberystwyth in 1828 and traded regularly with Liverpool until the railway arrived. She was eventually wrecked c1869.
(Posters XHE 'A')

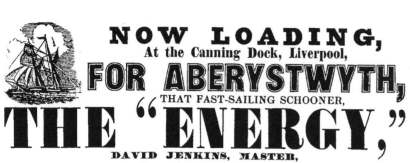

NOW LOADING,

At the Canning Dock, Liverpool,

FOR ABERYSTWYTH,

THAT FAST-SAILING SCHOONER,

THE "ENERGY,"

DAVID JENKINS, MASTER,

And will positively Sail on or before the

Goods taken in for the following Places:

ABERAYRON	GOGINAN	LLANIDLOES	LLANSANTFFREAD	PENROCK	TRE'RDDOL,
BORTH	LAMPETER	LLANILAR	PONTERWYD	RHAYADER	AND
CWMYSTWYTH	LLANDDEWIBREFI	LLANNON	PONTRHYDFENDIGAID	TALYBONT	PLACES
DEVIL'S BRIDGE	LLANGEITHO	LLANRHYSTID	PONTRHYDYGROES	TREGARON	ADJACENT.

☞ *For Freight apply to the Captain on Board, or to Capt. Evan Jenkins, 37, Portland Street, Aberystwyth.*

EVAN JENKINS returns his grateful thanks to his Friends and the Public, for the kind patronage so long extended to the "Energy," and humbly solicits a continuance of the same, which, by the strictest care and attention, it will be his constant endeavour to merit.

E. WILLIAMS AND SON, PRINTERS, ABERYSTWYTH.

The 62 ton schooner *Energy* was built in Aberystwyth in 1844 and traded regularly with Liverpool. She was eventually sold to Belfast owners in 1871.
(Posters XHE 'A'))

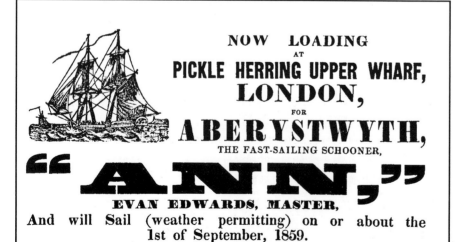

NOW LOADING

AT

PICKLE HERRING UPPER WHARF,

LONDON,

FOR

ABERYSTWYTH,

THE FAST-SAILING SCHOONER,

"ANN,"

EVAN EDWARDS, MASTER,

And will Sail (weather permitting) on or about the 1st of September, 1859.

D. JENKINS, PRINTER, PIER STREET, ABERYSTWYTH.

Ann, a 39 ton schooner built at Bideford in 1830 sailed from Aberystwyth to London until the railway arrived and put her out of business. (Posters XHE 'A')

voyages. There were on average 8 - 10 shipments of timber per year from north America alone and it was not unusual for Aberystwyth vessels to meet up in these ports. On one occasion in 1874 both *Hope* and *Wellington* left Darien in Georgia, then a major source of pitch pine, on the same day and raced each other back to Aberystwyth. This trade was not without its dangers and casualties. *Rhydol* was abandoned after hitting an iceberg in 1845, *Credo* had to be abandoned in mid-Atlantic in 1872, whilst *Hope* capsized with the loss of 5 lives in a hurricane 200 miles off the Canadian coast in 1892 when carrying a cargo of timber for Porthmadog. Many problems encountered by timber carrying ships resulted from carrying quantities of cargo on deck. In rough weather this was likely to break free hampering the crew and damaging the deck fittings.

Most of the imported timber was destined for two timberyards. One was in Trefechan and belonged to the Roberts family and later sold to Meggit & Jones whilst the second was on the site now covered by South Marine Terrace and Rheidol Terrace. This was kept by Thomas Jones. The timber trade continued until the 1920s though after the 1880s the demand decreased as both shipbuilding and lead mining declined. Consequently the transatlantic trade in timber which had focussed on Darien, Quebec and ports such as Dalhousie, Bathurst and Miramichi on the eastern seaboard of Canada ceased and what timber was needed came from Scandinavia

ABERYSTWYTH
And Cardigan Bay
STEAM PACKET COMPANY
(LIMITED.)

18  **66.**

The above Company, formed by the Gentlemen and Tradesmen of Aberystwyth and its Vicinity, beg leave to inform the Public, that their

POWERFUL SCREW STEAMER
EXPRESS

JAMES DAVIES, COMMANDER,

will leave Aberystwyth regularly every Monday, and will return from Liverpool and Bristol alternately every Friday,---casualties excepted,---as follows,---

FROM BRISTOL FOR ABERYSTWYTH.				FROM LIVERPOOL FOR ABERYSTWYTH.			
Friday, January	5th	Friday, April	13th	Friday, January	12th	Friday, April	6th
,, ,,	19th	,, ,,	27th	,, ,,	26th	,, ,,	20th
,, February	2nd	,, May	11th	,, February	9th	,, May	4th
,, ,,	16th	,, ,,	25th	,, ,,	23rd	,, ,,	18th
,, March	2nd	,, June	8th	,, March	9th	,, June	1st
,, ,,	16th	,, ,,	22nd	,, ,,	23rd	,, ,,	15th
,, ,,	30th					,, ,,	29th

For Rates of Freight, apply to the Agents, D. W. DAVIES, Washington Buildings, Brunswick Street, Liverpool; MARK WHITWILL & SON, Grove, Bristol; and WILLIAM JONES, 14, North Parade, Aberystwyth.

Loading Berth at LIVERPOOL, VICTORIA DOCK. Loading Berth at BRISTOL, WELSH BACK.

NOTICE TO SHIPPERS.

The above Company receive all Goods on the Conditions and Agreement only of shipping them under a bill of lading or receipt, in the form adopted by the Company; and if from any cause whatsoever, Goods shall be shipped without a bill of lading or receipt, the Company are only liable to convey and deliver the same on the terms of the bill of lading or receipt adopted by them, namely, "That this Vessel have leave to sail with or without a Pilot, to touch and stay at intermediate Ports, with liberty to tow and assist Vessels, and that the Company or Agents have power to tranship the said Goods, or to ship them by first and following Vessels after receiving them, and are not liable for inward condition, leakage, or breakages, contents or weight of packages, nor the incorrect delivery of Goods from the insufficiency of marks or numbers, nor for any accident, loss, or damage, arising from the act of God, the Queen's enemies, pirates, restraints of Princes, Rulers, and People, jettison, barratry, collision, fire on board, damage by vermin, fire or robbery in bulk, craft, shed, or store, or on shore, nor from any accident, loss, or damage whatsoever from machinery, boilers, and steam, and steam navigation, nor from any peril of the seas and rivers, nor from any act, neglect or default whatsoever of the pilot, master, or crew, nor from any consequences of the causes above stated." And further, if the Goods are, for the convenience of Shippers or Consignees, booked through or addressed for any place beyond the aforesaid port of Steamer's destination, that the Company shall not be held accountable for any loss or damage to the said Goods; or for any delay in their transmission or delivery; or be in any respect liable for whatsoever may happen to them, after being landed on the quay or wharf, or discharged into hulk or craft, at the aforesaid port.
No claims for deficiency or damage to Goods will be allowed unless observed before removal from the Vessel, the Carrier's receipt for the Goods in good order, clearing the ship from any damage, deficiency, or liability. All Goods must be removed when landed, otherwise they remain entirely at their owners' risk.

PHILIP WILLIAMS, PRINTER & STATIONER, BRIDGE STREET, ABERYSTWYTH.

The **Aberystwyth and Cardigan Bay Steam Packet Company** was formed in 1863. It owned the *Express* before purchasing the *Henry E Taylor*. The company later evolved into the **Aberystwyth & Aberdovey Steam Packet Company**, discussed elsewhere in the book.
(Posters, XHE)

Unloading timber from an unidentified vessel, c1870.   (Photo Album 1262, PZ5463/81)

The harbour c1865, with various small vessels in the course of construction below South Road
or Shipbuilders Row as it was known until the start of the twentieth century.
(Photo Album 805, PA7165)

The launch of any vessel was a big occasion almost akin to a public holiday. The account from the *Aberystwyth Observer* of the launch of *Sir Robert McClure* gives some indication of the proceedings.

"On Saturday the 17th instant [March 1866] a fine clipper modelled brig named the Sir Robert McClure classed A1 twelve years at Lloyds, burden 350 tons was launched from the yard of Mr John Evans. She is fitted up with the latest and most superior improvements; and is to be employed in the southern trade. She will be commanded by Mr Ellis Griffiths, who is also a large shareholder. The ship has been named as a graceful compliment after the celebrated Arctic navigator under whose command Capt Griffiths served as an A B for four years during one of his expeditions from 1854 to 1859. Capt Griffiths has since commanded in the Black Ball Line, of Liverpool. This reflects great credit on the energy and worth of the captain. The ceremony of christening the vessel was performed by the lady of Mr John Jones, manager of the North & South Wales Bank, of this town."

The launching of a ship always attracted a crowd of people, especially children who would congregate to watch the customary bottle of port smash against the hull and the vessel glide gracefully into the water. It was a common practice for a religious service to be held aboard the vessel just after launching., All workers involved were afterwards treated to a celebratory meal, courtesy of their employers

The brig Sir Robert McClure on the stocks, c1866.

(Photo Album 1393, PZ5927/1)

Aberystwyth Harbour, c1870.   (Photo Album 1262 PZ5463/84)

Aberystwyth Harbour c1865 with three vessels on the stocks.   (Photo Album 1262, PZ5463/13)

AN ERA OF DECLINE

Just as the decades leading up to the arrival of the railway had been a prosperous era for the harbour so the decades that followed its arrival were ones of decline. Much of the freight that once came in the holds of coasting schooners now arrived by train - swiftly, conveniently and usually on time; neither did goods bought by rail suffer the same degree of breakages as their ocean-going counterparts. After this date imports tended to be bulky items such as coal, grain, bricks, and in particular, timber. Severe storms damaged the stone pier in 1867 making the need for rapid repairs imperative. Harbour dues had been reduced by the arrival of the railway and were insufficient to cover both the repair work and the interest due on the original loan. The eventual result of this was that control of the harbour passed to Aberystwyth Town Council in 1874. As illustrated in the case of the *Fairy* (discussed elsewhere) the harbour was neglected and in need of routine maintenance.

Shipbuilding continued with many fine vessels leaving the stocks at Aberystwyth, the majority being schooners of about 100 tons. Larger

Fishing boats in the inner harbour c1895.

(Photo album 833, PB2340)

The hulk of *Sarah Davies*, built in Derwenlas in 1860 slowly rots away in the harbour, c1910. (Photo Album 1275, PZ5476/31)

vessels traded far and wide; The 285 ton *Lady Pryse,* launched in 1875 was one of a number of Aberystwyth vessels to visit South Africa. Shipbuilding dwindled as the 1870s wore on though 1878 saw a slight renaissance with three launches - *Nerissa, Rheidol* and *Caroline Spooner.* The 663 ton *Caroline Spooner* was the largest built in the port. She was captained by John Hughes of Borth and usually crewed by a mixed bunch in more ways than one and it was a rare occasion for her to leave port without leaving at least one crew member behind in either a hospital or prison. *Caroline Spooner* was eventually condemned in Chile in 1895. She was sold to new owners who christened her *Oceola*. She sank two years later, perhaps a vindication of the sailors

adage that it was unlucky to change the name of a ship.

The last ship to be built in Aberystwyth was the *Edith Eleanor*, (discussed elsewhere) launched in 1881 for timber merchant D C Roberts.

The area used for shipbuilding was walled in during the 1890s once it became obvious that no more ships were to be built there. However to provide a shelter for fishing boats a small inner harbour, known to all and sundry as "The Gap", was created.

The year 1886 saw a further change in the appearance of the harbour with Trefechan bridge being washed away in a flood that caused immense damage elsewhere in the town. Work on its replacement, which still stands today, was started the following year.

SOME EXAMPLES OF ABERYSTWYTH SHIPPING

Crew agreements for vessels registered at Aberystwyth from 1863 to 1913 are to be found in the National Library of Wales. These agreements list the crew, duration of voyages and ports of call for each ship. Occasionally other information, such as cargoes carried can also be gleaned. The number of vessels for which these agreements exist approaches six hundred, an indication of the prosperity shipping brought to the town. Sheer numbers make it difficult to generalise as to the nature of the vessels themselves, the trades in which they were involved, or almost any aspect of their careers. Sailing vessels ranged in size from small fishing boats of less than ten tons to Cape Horners such as the *Caradoc, General Nott* and *General Picton*, which were far too large to even consider entering their home port. The only observation that can be made with any certainty is that the larger the vessel the farther it was likely to roam. Even this statement decries the fact that many of the small vessels travelled great distances. Schooners of 100 or so tons were regularly employed in the Mediterranean trade and also crossed the Atlantic to Canada. Britain's insatiable demand for sugar took slightly larger vessels such as *J Llywelyn*, a 161 ton barquentine built in Aberystwyth in 1869 to the warmer climes of the Caribbean. Under a tropical sun, in the shadow of the twin Pitons at Soufriere, riding at anchor off the palm fringed beaches of Barbados

sugar was loaded for refineries in London and Glasgow to eventually sweeten innumerable cups of tea and coffee. The same trade took her and many others beside to Berbice, Guyana and the steaming jungles of South America. Another far flung corner of the empire that claimed the attention of Aberystwyth vessels during the 1870s was Port Alfred in South Africa, a destination for all manner of goods from gunpowder to sewing machines.

The Cape Horners were usually involved in importing either guano or copper ore from Chile for which Valparaiso was the main port. The demand for these products was heavy, so consequently vessels may have had to wait at anchor in the bay for many weeks for their turn to load. Shore leave was not generally given as Valparaiso was notorious for its dockside bars, inhabited by crimps eager to kidnap and sell unwary sailors to unscrupulous captains in need of a crew.

The largest ships registered at Aberystwyth were the tramp steamers of the Cambrian Steam Navigation Co Ltd. Hopefully the brief surveys of individual vessels given here will shed some light on the diversity and activities of the town's fleet, whilst the section on John Mathias summarises this aspect of Aberystwyth shipping.

The quality of workmanship exhibited in the construction of wooden vessels and the fastidious care lavished on them

under their proud owners ensured that some survived well on into the present century. The largest vessel to be built in the town to survive into this century was the 362 ton *Ivanhoe* built in 1871 and sold to Hamburg owners whilst in Portugal in 1898. Her final fate is still unknown though she was still listed as being in A1 condition in 1900.

With the exception of the *Eliza Francis*, whom we will meet later, all other Aberystwyth built vessels had been sold and re-registered at other ports by 1919 making their stories harder to piece together. The port of registry can be misleading; *Confidence* was re-registered in Beaumaris in 1881 but spent her later years under Arklow owners, to be deleted from the shipping registers in 1907 after being declared a constructive total wreck. The year 1911 saw a further three vessels deleted from the registers. *Blue Jacket*, by now over 50 years old and registered at Caernarfon had the indignity of being broken up. Wreckage from *Fanny Fothergill* (built in Aberystwyth in 1865, subsequently re-registered at Fleetwood) was found 100 miles North North West of Land's End. There was no sign of her crew of six. *Desdemona* was lost in October of the same year. It is worthy of note that until late 1995 there was a house in North Parade, Aberystwyth called *Desdemona* after the schooner of the same name. Perhaps the saddest end of all the remaining Aber vessels was the *Glad Tidings* which disappeared without trace on a stormy night in February 1914, laden with a cargo of coal from Garston and bound for her adopted port of Drogheda. The crew comprised the owner Captain Whitehead, his three sons and a young boy called Owens on his first voyage. In Drogheda a Disaster Fund was instigated for the relief of the captain's widow, her four children and the family of young Owens.

Enemy action claimed three sailing vessels with Aberystwyth connections in the first world war, all as a consequence of U-boat attacks. The first was *Utopia* a 184 ton brig registered at Aberystwyth from 1860 - 1911. She was sunk along with another sailing vessel by gunfire from a U-boat 20 miles off Dungeness on March 2nd 1917. The following month *Agnes Cairns* which was registered at Aberystwyth during the 1880s and 1890s was captured and sunk eight miles north east of Alderney. The third casualty, *Acorn, was* built in Aberdyfi in 1864 and sunk on September 26th 1917, approximately twenty miles south east of Start Point, near Plymouth. *Raymond*, a 188 ton Canadian built brigantine associated with Aberystwyth from 1877 to c1895 was more fortunate. She too was attacked by a U-boat off Ushant, but a timely intervention saved her from destruction. All the vessels were unarmed at the time and no lives were lost. The war years also claimed *Morning Star*, wrecked near Dunabrattan in 1915.

By 1918 only four vessels built in Aberystwyth viz *Edith Eleanor* (discussed further on), *Ellen Beatrice*, *Eliza Francis* and *Meridian* were still in existence.

Coincidentally the last two were both captained by Richard Francis at some stage in their careers. *Meridian*, by now registered at Bridgwater, was wrecked in 1920. *Ellen Beatrice*, by now registered at Weymouth, survived her by three years before being broken up after carrying coastal cargoes for 59 years.

This leaves *Eliza Francis* built in 1852 as the last surviving Aberystwyth-built sailing ship. She disappears from the records c1925. It seems that the last years of her working life were spent on Merseyside as her penultimate owners were Buchanans Flour Mills who sold her to Alfred H Connell of 17 Water Street, Liverpool. Due to her age it is quite likely that she was scrapped or converted into a lighter.

The 141 ton brig *Truant* was built in Aberystwyth in 1840. She was lost with all hands in 1874.
(Original Drawings, PE5843)

A sloop probably *John & Mary* in trouble at the harbour mouth, c1848.   (Welsh Primitive, Carmarthen Museum)

John & Mary

John & Mary was a 44 ton sloop built in the Lerry Boatyard, Borth in 1842 and typical of the vessels using the harbour at the time. She was named after the captain's parents. The tragedy depicted in this sketch occured on 9th February 1848. The vessel was carrying a cargo of culm (fine coal) from Neath to Aberdyfi but heavy seas had damaged her steering gear and she tried to put in at Aberystwyth. Unable to negotiate the harbour entrance properly in the stormy conditions prevailing she grounded on Ro-fawr only ten yards from shore and quickly keeled over onto one side. Captain Evan Hughes, a member of the Wesleyan chapel at Borth, is seen dangling from a rope. He was drowned when the vessel lurched further on her side, the hatch gave way and the cargo spilled out on top of him. The mate was also drowned. The two men in the rigging were both saved. One managed to climb to the end of the mast and jump to shore, by now suspended over the beach while a rescue party reached the other.

Volunteer at Aberdyfi, c1885.

(John Thomas Collection B18)

Volunteer

The 64 ton schooner *Volunteer* was built locally and owned for many years by Captain Edward Jones of Powell Street. She is typical of the type of vessel built at Aberystwyth during the middle of the nineteenth century. Launched in 1861 and immediately put into use in the coasting trade Volunteer carried numerous small cargoes during the course of the next half century. A typical six month period in 1864 involved voyages from Barrow, Port Talbot, Aberystwyth, Greenfield, Bagillt, Dundalk, Cardiff and Aberystwyth. Her visits to Aberystwyth brought timber, grain, coal or bricks. She was a familiar sight at many ports until her sale to new owners in the Isles of Scilly in 1908 who used her to transport coal from south Wales to the Scillies. She foundered in the Bristol Channel in 1910. Some parts of the vessel were salvaged including the figurehead which is to be seen in the figurehead collection at Valhalla, Tresco and thought to be the only such relic from an Aberystwyth built vessel to have survived. Her size and the nature of her trade make her representative of a large number of vessels associated with the town.

The 179 ton brig *Fanny Fothergill*, c1870 as depicted by a pierhead artist.   (Album 1695, PZ6811/25)

Fanny Fothergill

Launched in Aberystwyth in 1865 for her owner and master John Hughes of Terrace Road *Fanny Fothergill* was registered in the town for twenty years before being sold to Fleetwood owners. She frequently traded between Genoa and Antwerp and also between ports in South America such as Berbice and Demerara carrying sugar for either London or Glasgow. However on one notable voyage commencing in September 1874 she sailed from London for South Africa and onto the Seychelles, Sri Lanka, India, Australia and New Zealand before returning to Liverpool in May 1877. She foundered with all hands in 1911.

Edith Eleanor in the Bay of Naples, c1885 by Roberto Luigi.   (Framed Works, PG0513)

Edith Eleanor

The last wooden sailing ship to be built in Aberystwyth, the 96 ton schooner *Edith Eleanor,* was launched in 1881 for timber merchant D C Roberts. From her rig and size she would be expected have been involved primarily in the coasting trade, though as the above picture shows she sailed far and wide in search of cargoes. In 1885 she made the following round trip: Porthmadog to Hamburg with slates, to Cadiz in ballast, across the Atlantic to Labrador with salt, on to Naples with a cargo of salt fish, in ballast to St Vaas (France) where she loaded with salt for Penzance and back to Porthmadog in ballast during the space of eleven months. This involved a distance of some 11,650 miles, the longest leg (Labrador to Naples) being 4000 miles. The crew for this voyage totalled five including captain and ships boy. The crew were also responsible for loading and unloading all cargoes. *Edith Eleanor* was re-registered at Wexford in 1916 and eventually lost in 1921.

Painting of Fairy.   (Framed Work, PB8181)

Fairy

A three masted brigantine built in Littlehampton in 1864 *Fairy*, was acquired by local businessman and cooper John Jones of Trefechan in 1878. She is known to have traded with Rosario, Barcelona and London. Her fate was decided not by stormy seas or high winds but in her home port of Aberystwyth. Whilst moored in the harbour her mooring ring came adrift and the vessel was severely damaged. Her owner accused the Town Council of negligence and took them to court, resulting in a journey of far greater duration than any of her voyages across the seven seas. *Fairy* navigated a tortuous passage through the judicial system via the Swansea Assizes and susequent hearings in London. The matter was settled out of court with the council paying £1300 to John Jones. Valued at £196 *Fairy* was subsequently broken up in 1882 and anything saleable auctioned off.

Hind at an Irish port c1885.

(Photo Album 973, PZ5159/32)

Hind

Hind was a 115 ton brigantine built in Cardiff in 1862 and registered at Aberystwyth from 1879 - 1888. Although registered here her loyalty was to New Quay from where Captain Phillips and many of his crew came from. As indicated in the photo at times she traded between the south Wales coal ports and Irish ports. Like the similar sized *Edith Eleanor* she also traded between the Mediterranean and Canada. On April 28th 1887 she left Swansea with a crew of six for Lisbon carrying coal. At Cadiz she loaded up with a cargo of salt from where she departed on 26th May for Newfoundland. Arriving on 23rd July, *Hind* did not depart from Newfoundland until 11th November and took 32 days to cross the Atlantic and reach Gibraltar. Her cargo would have been barrels of saltfish. After unloading the cargo of fish at Alicante and loading a new cargo the voyage finally ended at Stockton on Tees on 28th March 1888. Handling all cargoes and ballast was also part of the crew's responsibility. She was sold later the same year.

Hope alongside St Davids Quay, c1890.

(Photo Album 1262, PZ5463/27)

Hope

Built by Pierre Labbie of Quebec in 1865 the 275 ton barque *Hope* was acquired by Aberystwyth timber merchant Thomas Jones in 1871. Although Canadian vessels cost only half the price of their British counterparts they were only reckoned to half their life span. Until 1884 she was involved solely in importing timber from Canada, Scandinavia and the port of Darien in Georgia. In 1874 *Hope* and another Aberystwyth vessel *Wellington* left Darien on the same day. Racing across the Atlantic *Wellington* arrived home in 31 days, three days ahead of *Hope*. After 1884 her trading pattern changed. Aberystwyth no longer sought the large quantities of timber used in shipbuilding. Instead *Hope* was engaged in importing

timber to other ports including Rhyl, Porthmadog and Douglas. Occasionally she now carried outward cargoes of coal to coaling stations including Madeira and Dakar.

Altogether *Hope* crossed the Atlantic sixty nine times. Her end came when she encountered a hurricane sixty miles from Cape Race, Canada. Hit by tumultous storms she started to take in water. To lighten the load the crew tried to jettison the deck cargo. Before this was achieved the vessel capsized. Most of the crew climbed on to the upturned hull but were later washed off. Four days later three of the crew were picked up by a fishing boat, the other five having been lost.

The 1350 ton *Caradoc* photographed at an unidentified port, c1900.   (Photo Album 1392, PZ5926/75)

Caradoc

A steel hulled three masted barque built in Sunderland in 1891, *Caradoc* was the largest sailing vessel registered at Aberystwyth. Owned locally, she was involved in the importation of Guano from the Pacific coast of South America to Hamburg and Antwerp, a trip involving a return journey around Cape Horn that could last over a year. Author Hans de Mierre encountered *Caradoc* in Newcastle, New South Wales, and noted that many of her crew were related and as much Welsh as English was spoken aboard. She was captained for many years by Lewis Williams of Borth and later by David Jones of Aberystwyth. In October 1897 *Caradoc* came across the Norwegian vessel *Caledonia* in a sinking state and despite heavy seas rescued seven seamen. This act was recognised by the Norwegian government who honoured the captain and the first and second mates with bravery awards.

ABERYSTWYTH & ABERDOVEY STEAM PACKET CO. LTD.

This local company evolved from the similarly named **Aberystwyth & Cardigan Bay Steam Packet Co Ltd**. The company operated a regular steamer service between Aberystwyth and Liverpool, importing a variety of items for tradesmen and farmers in the neighbourhood and exporting lead ore. Like its predecesor it operated the steamer *Henry E Taylor* which traded regularly between Liverpool and Aberystwyth. The vessel, named after Henry Enfield Taylor a local entrepreneur, was built in 1868 specifically for the company. In April 1886 onlookers at the harbour saw the familiar smudge of

smoke on the horizon evolve not into the familiar shape of the *Henry E Taylor* but the brand new *Countess of Lisburne*, built at Grangemouth specifically for the company. The *Countess* continued in the tradition of her predecessor with three voyages a month between Liverpool and Aberystwyth with occasional calls to other north Wales ports such as Pwllheli and Abermo. As a result of her heavy iron hull the Countess was becoming as much of a liability as an asset and was eventually sold in 1908. Her new owners re-christened her *Sao Vicente* and sailed her across the Atlantic Ocean. She eventually foundered six years later in a

tributary of the River Amazon. Her replacement was the *Grosvenor*, a second hand but relatively new vessel capable of carrying far more cargo. Her last visit to the town was in August 1915 as the following month she was sold. Communications between Aberystwyth and Liverpool were maintained by the "Aberdovey & Barmouth Steamship Co" vessel *Dora* until October 1916. The combined effects of the First World War and increasing competition from the railways proved too much for the company and in 1916 the company was wound up.

Aberystwyth Harbour c1885. The *Henry E Taylor* is moored on the right of the picture. (Photo Album 2145, PG6395)

THE
ABERYSTWYTH & ABERDOVEY
STEAM PACKET CO., Ltd.

THE

"Countess of Lisburne"

(Weather and other circumstances permitting, with liberty to tow and assist vessels,)
OR OTHER STEAMER, will (until further notice) SAIL FROM
LIVERPOOL.

LOADING BERTH—WEST SIDE TRAFALGAR LOCK.

The address of the Consignee, with the port of destination, to be distinctly marked on each package, and all sacks must be properly stitched, otherwise the Company will not be responsible, nor be accountable for the correct delivery. Correct weight of all goods to be stated on Shipping Notes by Shippers. Petroleum Oil and other explosives received on day of sailing only.

Fares, Cabin 5/-; Return 7/6. Fore Deck 3/-; Return 4/6.
AVAILABLE FOR ONE MONTH AND NOT TRANSFERABLE.

THREE TIMES A MONTH FOR ABERSTWYTH, receiving Goods up to Noon each day of sailing, as follows :—

	JULY		AUG.		SEPT.		OCT.		NOV.		DEC.	
1895.	JULY	5	AUG.	2	SEPT.	6	OCT.	4	NOV.	1	DEC.	13
	,,	12	,,	9	,,	20	,,	18	,,	15	,,	20
	,,	26	,,	23	,,	27	,,	25	,,	22	,,	27
			,,	30					,,	29		

For Rates of Freight, and other particulars, apply to

ROBERT OWEN,
27, Water Street, LIVERPOOL.
(TELEPHONE No. 1.855.)
Telegraphic Address: " MERION," Liverpool.

OR TO

Mr. ISAAC GRIFFITHS,
Steam Packet Co., ABERYSTWYTH.

Poster advertising the services of the *Countess of Lisburne*, c1900.
XHE 'A')

(Posters,

Countess of Lisburne in Aberystwyth
Harbour, c1905.
(Photo Album 833, PZ7264)

Passengers as well as cargo could be
carried aboard the *Countess*.
(Photo Album 1272, PZ5473/3)

Slates were a relatively fragile cargo and had to be handled with care as this view from c1908 shows.
(Photo Album 1272, PZ5473/85)

Grosvenor at the quayside, c1910. Note the narrow gauge rails, an extension of the Vale of Rheidol line.
(Photo Album 1275, PZ5476/55)

JOHN MATHIAS & THE CAMBRIAN STEAM NAVIGATION COMPANY

The largest vessels connected with Aberystwyth were a fleet of tramp steamers owned by the Cambrian Steam Navigation Company Limited and engaged primarily in taking South Wales coal to coaling stations worldwide. Despite recruiting local seamen and being registered at Aberystwyth, these vessels never visited the town as they were far too big to enter the harbour. John Mathias (1837 - 1912), was born locally and by 1868 was running a grocery business in Bridge Street. Like most businesses in the town prior to the arrival of the railway he relied on goods imported by sea and like so many of the town's merchants, mariners and businessmen started to invest in shipping. The first vessel he owned outright was *Miss Evans* bought in 1869. He later bought *Solway,* a 177 ton brig launched in Aberystwyth in 1868 and wrecked off the coast of Morrocco in 1885. However the age of the small sailing vessel was drawing to a close. John Mathias decided to use his expertise in shipping and entrepreneurial skills to commission the building of the 1,005 ton steamer *Glanrheidol.* This was achieved by establishing a single ship company called "The Glanrheidol Steamship Co." formed in 1883 with the backing of a number of local shareholders.

Glanrheidol was managed by Mathias, crewed by a large contingent of Borth and Aberystwyth seamen and employed primarily in the south Wales coal trade. It is worth mentioning the similarities between *Glanrheidol* and another vessel with Aberystwyth connections, the 980 ton *Glanwern.* This latter vessel was

THE CAMBRIAN STEAM NAVIGATION COMPANY, LIMITED.

Managers:
J. MATHIAS & SONS.

Secretary:
T. D. JENKINS.

Company's Registered Office:
BALTIC CHAMBERS, ABERYSTWYTH.

Their house flag was the Prince of Wales feathers in a red diamond on a blue background.
(NLW Printed Books)

launched in March 1882 and owned by the "Aberystwith Steamship Company", itself a locally based single ship company. It is possible that the success of this venture inspired Mathias to undertake his own enterprise as both vessels were built at the same shipyard (W. Doxford & Sons of Sunderland), both had similar tonnages and both had the pre-fix *Glan.* Over the next few years Mathias repeated the process with *Glanystwyth, Glanayron, Glanhafren* and *Glantivy.* The last two were second hand rather than newly built vessels. As time progressed and his reputation grew, the need to stress the local aspect of his ventures receded. Head Office was still in Baltic Chambers, Terrace Road, Aberystwyth (opposite "Barclays Bank") and local seamen were still sought as crew members but the local connection in the naming of ships ceased. In 1896 the Cambrian Steam Navigation Co Ltd was formed and became Mathias's flagship company, passing to his sons after his death. His other single ship companies were wound up and vessels either sold or transferred to the new company which became known unofficially as the College Line due to the names of its ships. At its peak in 1906-7 the fleet stood at eight vessels, all of at least 3,000 gross registered tonnage. In

1914 the company was the eighth largest of seventy Cardiff based shipping companies with a fleet of six vessels, three of which were later lost as a result of enemy action. After the end of the war the decision to wind up the company's activities, now limited to two vessels *Northern* and *Western*, was taken and the remaining vessels sold. "The Cambrian Steam Navigation Co." was wound up in 1924.

165.

THE CAMBRIAN STEAM NAVIGATION Co., LD.

MOVEMENTS OF STEAMERS
during May, 1910.

Cheltonian—
4	Left Barrow for Barry Dock.
6	Arrived Barry Dock.
12	Left Barry Dock for Naples.
24	Arrived Naples.
31	Left Naples for Barry Roads (for orders).

Cliftonian—
1	Arrived Naples.
10	Left Naples for Odessa.
17	Arrived Odessa.
28	Left Odessa for London.

Harrovian—
5	Arrived Hamburg.
20	Left Hamburg for Cardiff.
24	Arrived Cardiff.

Etonian—
1	Arrived Cardiff.
10	Left Cardiff for Port Said.
25	Arrived Port Said.

Rugbeian—
3	Left Marseilles for Seville.
8	Arrived Seville.
15	Left Seville for Lisbon.
17	Arrived Lisbon.
19	Left Lisbon for New York.

Carthusian—
10	Arrived Rotterdam.
14	Left Rotterdam for Newport (Mon.)
16	Arrived Newport (Mon.)
25	Left Newport (Mon.) for Malta.

Breconian—
3	Left Achtari for Brake.
21	Arrived Brake.

J. MATHIAS & SONS,
MANAGERS.

198.

THE CAMBRIAN STEAM NAVIGATION Co., LD.

MOVEMENTS OF STEAMERS
during February, 1913.

Harrovian—
10	Arrived Naples.
26	Left Naples for Marseilles.
28	Arrived Marseilles.

Etonian—
6	Left Naples for Barry Dock.
16	Arrived Barry Dock.

Rugbeian—
8	Left Fiume for Cardiff.
21	Arrived Cardiff.

Carthusian—
10	Passed Monte Video for Carthagena.

Breconian—
	On Indian Coast Trade.

Cliftonian—
5	Arrived Rotterdam.
9	Left Rotterdam for Barry Dock.
12	Arrived Barry Dock.
22	Left Barry Dock for Alexandria.

Cheltonian—
7	Passed Norfolk Va.
24	Arrived Bremerhaven.

J. MATHIAS & SONS,
MANAGERS.

The activities of the company's fleet is best summarised by two of the regular bulletins issued by the company. (NLW Printed Books)

SS *Harrovian* 5,555 grt was built in 1914 and lost in 1916. The well deck between the forecastle and bridge distinguish her from her predecessor.

(Photo Album 1262, PZ5463/45)

Reference No.	SIGNATURES OF CREW.	Age.	*Nationality. (If British, state birthplace.)	PARTICULAR	
				Ship in which he last served, and Year of Discharge therefrom.	
				Year.	State Name and Official No. or Port she belonged to.
	1	2	3	4	5
1	R. James *Master to sign first.*	40	Borth	1901	*Feliciana* *Aberystwyth*
2	J R Brown	35	Aberystwyth	1900	*Glanhafren* *Aberystwyth*
3	Evan Hughes	33	Portmadoc	1901	
4	Thomas Clayton	49	Aberystwyth	1901	*Feliciana* *Aberystwyth*
5	William Thomas	51	Llanelly	1901	*Feliciana* *Aberystwyth*
6	L B Lewis	27	Aberystwyth	1900	*George* *Isle of Ramsey*

A portion of the crew agreement for *Harrovian* for a voyage in 1901 underlining the connection between the company and Aberystwyth.

(MSS Aberystwyth Shipping Records)

A portion of the crew agreement for Glanhafren in 1893 showing the local links between the Cambrian Steam Navigation Co Ltd and Ceredigion.
(NLW MSS, Aberystwyth Shipping Records)

Reference No.	SIGNATURES OF CREW.	Year of Birth.	Town or County where born.	If in the Reserve, No. of Commission or R. V. 2.	Ship in which he last served, and Year of Discharge therefrom.		Date and this
					Year.	State Name and Official No. or Port she belonged to.	Date.
	1		2	3	4	5	6	7
1	Thomas Walters *Master to sign first.*	43	Newquay			Same	8.9.93
2	John Hughes	36	Borth			,	,
3	Richard Jones	57	do			,	,
4	John Jones	36	do			,	,
5	Thomas Boughton	35	A'wyth			,	,
6	William Thomas	39	do			,	,

Captain Walters of New Quay and the crew of Glanhafren in Huelva, Spain in 1894. The captain's wife frequently served as stewardess.
(Photo Album 2145 199600085)

Steamships managed by J Mathias & Son.

Single Ship Companies

Glan Steamship Company Ltd
Venus, launched 1891 Stockton, 2940 grt. Foundered after a collision near Beachy Head , June 1899 within three months of acquisition by the company.

Glanayron Steamship Co Ltd
Glanayron, (ex *Santon*) launched July 1889, 2504 grt . Wrecked May 1896.

Glanhafren Steamship Co Ltd
Glanhafren, (ex *Harperly*) launched May 1888, South Shields, 2233 grt. Wrecked off Tunisian coast without loss of life, 1903.

Glanrheidol Steamship Co Ltd
Glanrheidol, launched 1883, 1005 grt. Sold 1891 and renamed *Newbiggin* (later *Arosa*).

Glantivy Steamship Co Ltd
Glantivy (*ex Alton Tower*) launched March 1891, 2949 grt.

Glanystwyth Steamship Co Ltd
Glanystwyth launched 1888, Newcastle 1824 grt. Sold 1897 and renamed *Girda-Ambatiellos.*

Cambrian Steam Navigation Co Ltd

(J Mathias & Sons Ltd, Managers)
Breconian, launched 1906, Doxford & Sons, Sunderland 4121 grt. Sold out of fleet, 1917.
Carthusian, launched 1905, Doxford & Sons, Sunderland 4121 grt.
Cheltonian #1, launched Dec 1892, Stockton 3084 grt as *Glenvech* and later renamed. Sold c1911 and renamed *Christos Markettos.*
Cheltonian #2, launched 1911 Bartram & Sons, Sunderland 4550 grt, sunk by gunfire from a German submarine 54 miles SW of Planier Lighthouse, near Marseilles, June 8 th 1917. Captain and one gunner taken prisoner.
Cliftonian #1, (ex *Strathisla*, ex *Pinedene,*) launched 1894, Newcastle, 3257 grt. Acquired c1899. Sold from fleet and renamed *Mar Cor.*
Cliftonian #2, launched 1911, Newcastle, 5,300 grt. Sunk by a German submarine near Galley Head, Southern Ireland, February 6th 1917 whilst in the service of the Royal Navy as a collier.
Etonian #1 (ex *Chicago*), launched 1898, Hartlepool, 6,438 grt. Acquired 1901 and sold to Leyland Line c1913. Sunk in Irish Sea by a German submarine, probably U-61 on March 23rd 1918 with the loss of 7 lives.
Etonian #2, launched Sunderland 1914, 4306 grt. Sold out of fleet c1918 and renamed *Clan Keith.*
Feliciana, launched Newcastle upon Tyne, 1891, 2922 grt. Acquired by the company in 1896. Sold from fleet April 1901.
Harrovian #1 (ex *Claverdale*) launched 1899, Newcastle, 3307 grt. Acquired c1903, sold out of fleet c1914 and renamed *Maurizio.*
Harrovian #2 built 1914, Sunderland 5,555 grt. Sunk by gunfire from a German U-boat 60 miles west of Bishop Rock, April 1916.
Northern, built 1912, Sunderland, 4731grt. Acquired c1917 to replace war losses and sold from fleet, 1920.
Reptonian (ex *Warfield*) 5,400 grt. Purchased c1904, sold c1909 and renamed *Caradoc.*
Rugbeian, launched 1904, Newcastle 6,800 grt. Sold out of fleet c1917, narrowly avoided being sunk by a German torpedo in the Mediterranean, June 1918.
Western (ex *War Fijian*) launched July 1918, Sunderland, 5225 grt. Managed on behalf of Fijian Ltd.

S S *Rugbeian*, the largest vessel owned by the Cambrian Steam Navigation Co Ltd.   (Photo Album 1391, PZ5925/76)

ABERYSTWYTH HARBOUR
TO 1945

The arrival of the twentieth century never threatened to restore the harbour to its former glory. Despite the activity to be seen in many turn of the century photographs the harbour was running at a loss of several hundred pounds per year. Regarded as a burden on the rates by some, competition from the harbour was instrumental in keeping rail freight charges at acceptable levels. Without competition from the harbour railway companies would have been free to charge as much as they liked for transporting goods to Aberystwyth. The cargoes that continued to arrive regularly were coal, timber, cement and fertiliser while lead ore continued to be shipped out, mainly in the *Countess of Lisburne.* With this trade in mind and for their own convenience the Vale of Rheidol railway built a branch line along the Rheidol, under Trefechan Bridge, around the Gap and along the town quay. This extension aided the offloading of the cargoes of rails imported by the contractors Messrs Pethick Bros, though how much use was ever made of this extension afterwards is debatable. It was closed in 1930.

Occasionally to be seen moored at the bottom of the harbour were vessels that never failed to command both respect and a wide berth from other harbour users. These were involved in importing explosives for use in the lead mines. Should an accident have befallen one of these vessels when entering the harbour the problem of silting at the harbour entrance could well have been solved once and for all.

A crane was erected on the quayside for unloading cargoes of Cornish Granite and Portland Stone to build the National Library of Wales. This arrived from 1911 until 1914 in vessels that included *Porthgain* of Bristol, *Fortuna* of Truro and *Forester* of Gloucester

The harbour at low water, c1900.

(Photo Album 1262, PZ5463/100).

An animated harbour view from c1902. The steamer at the quayside is the *Countess of Lisburne*. Also on view are some nobbies, a steam launch and a three masted sailing boat. Both the latter were used for taking visitors on trips in the bay. (Photo Album 2145, PG6165/1)

With the sale of the *Grosvenor* in 1915 and the winding up of the "Aberystwyth and Aberdovey Steam Packet Co Ltd" commercial usage of the harbour all but ceased. Any able bodied men were away on active service, many in the merchant navy and many through their previous links with the Royal Naval Reserve went into the Royal Navy, most notably on HMS Jupiter.

Following the arrival of the Irish schooner *Hilda* with a cargo of potatoes in 1917 no visits were made until 1921 when cargoes of potatoes, basic slag, cement and coal started to arrive. The following years saw a revival in trade but not on the scale of what went before. This can be illustrated by comparing the years 1907 and 1927.

The year 1907 saw a total of 73 visits by 19 different vessels. *Countess of Lisburne* called almost weekly, except for a five week period when in dock and her place taken by *Telephone* and *Dora*. Each of her visits brought 63 tons of general goods, whilst her substitutes managed an extra 10 and 13 tons respectively. Imports by other vessels included 7 cargoes totalling 673 tons of cement, 5 cargoes of coal totalling 370 tons, 4 cargoes totalling 673 tons of timber, 3 cargoes of manure (ie fertiliser) totalling 176 tons and two cargoes of stone totalling 129 tons. All except one of the outward cargoes went by the *Countess*. The exception was a shipment of ammonia, a by-product of the local gas plant which was shipped on *Telephone,* no doubt to the displeasure,

not to mention discomfort of her crew. Countess of Lisburne herself carried one such consignment during the year along with 17 cargoes of ore from lead mines in the Rheidol Valley, Cwmystwyth, Tal-y-bont and Strata Florida which totalled 1071 tons.

Twenty years later only 13 vessels visited the harbour importing 18 cargoes and exporting two. Six consignments each of coal (total 1150 tons) and manure / fertiliser (total 1123 tons) represented the most popular commodities. Four cargoes of stone totalling 655 tons arrived on *Garthloch* while one consignment each of cement (30 tons), macadam (165 tons) and 20,000 bricks completed the picture. Exports of zinc and lead ore concentrates totalled 780 tons for the year.

During the 1920s and 1930s a number of visits were paid to the harbour by vessels managed by Liverpool based Richard R Clark under the name of the "Overton Steamship Company". Characteristically the names of their vessels carried the suffix "-ton" and included *Beeston, Halton, Overton* and *Weston*. Overton was the first to visit the port carrying a cargo of 185 tons of basic slag for North Cardiganshire Farmers Co-operative in September 1924. Many of their subsequent cargoes were also of basic slag, the majority for David Rees & Co of Llanilar. These vessels had a gross tonnage of about 450 tons and could carry around 200 tons of cargo. Their design was typical for the era with the

bridge amidships rather than just in front of the funnel and the engine set back nearer the stern. The funnel was decorated with a distinctive 'O' denoting the name of the company. It was to this fleet that the ill-fated *Sutton* had belonged. After loading with a cargo of 400 tons of ore concentrates in late November 1925 she left for Antwerp, but after passing New Quay the cargo shifted and the vessel sank. Distress flares had been seen but were thought to be part of an exercise by some while others did not contact the authorities, resulting in the loss of fourteen lives.

Another vessel to visit the town, and in which R R Clark had an interest, was *Edern* owned by the Manchester,

Liverpool and North Wales Steamship Co of Liverpool. She arrived in November 1927 with a cargo of 450 tons of fertiliser.

Monroe Brothers were another company whose vessels frequently used the port. They had offices in both Liverpool and Cardiff and by 1926 ran a fleet of twelve steamships, noticably older than those of R R Clark. *Matje*, for example, had been built in 1890. She made one recorded visit in November 1927 with a mixed cargo of coal and 20,000 bricks for the Eastbrook Trading Co. *Dunvegan* collected a cargo of 320 tons of zinc ore in the same year. Visits from Monroe Brothers vessels ceased in 1928. This was a result of the company selling off it's smaller vessels and

Dating from c1905 this scene contains a number of fishing boats including *Plover*, moored against the quay on the left.

(Photo Album 833, PB5783)

The harbour entrance c1927. as seen from the capstan on the stone pier.
The wooden jetty was built in 1903-4 at a cost of some £16,000.
(Photo Album 706, PG221/100)

purchasing larger ships. Other Monroe Brothers vessels that visited Aberystwyth include *Edith, Nora, Jane* and *Ferrum,* usually with cargoes of coal.

Just as the interest of these two companies was waning, perhaps in part due to the danger posed by silting of the harbour mouth, a new breed of vessel started to appear. These were small motor vessels, often Dutch built, owned and crewed. They developed an uncanny ability to undercut rates charged by the steamers. Gradually visits by steamers became less frequent as coal, cement and roadstone arrived by motor vessel. The last steamer to bring in a cargo was *Accomac* in August 1939. The honours for the last steamer to use the port go to the ageing Isle of Man registered *Goldseeker* which arrived during the Second World War in desperate need of repair.

Unloading cargoes was still a laborious business in the 1930's.   (Photo Album 706, PG221/44)

All came to a halt in 1933 when the harbour was briefly frozen over.   (Photo Album 1262, PZ5463/23)

The schooner *Industry* was built in Gloucester and launched in December 1867. In 1917 she was acquired by John Davies of Borth who had fitted her with an auxiliary engine by the time she arrived in Aberystwyth in September 1921 with a cargo of coal. She was eventually wrecked on the Irish coast on November 27th 1921. This did not deter her owner from shipowning and over the next sixteen years he went on to own a further four vessels. His third vessel, the Aberystwyth registered *Plas Dinam* was a true tramp steamer, carrying cargoes to and from Canada, West Africa and the South Wales coal ports.

Industry in Aberystwyth Harbour, September 1921.
(Photo Album 833, PG8230/3)

Teddy 'the Ferry' James plies his trade in the foreground of this picture taken in August 1924. Behind him is the *Nordstjernen* unloading her cargo of timber.
(Photo Album1263, PZ5464/2)

Antigoon, a wooden auxiliary three masted schooner is seen discharging her cargo. On the horizon can be seen HMS *Diligence* and three destroyers.
(Photo Album 1275, PZ5476/35)

During the mid 1920s efforts were made to resurrect the importation of timber by sea. During the period 1924-6 four consignments of timber arrived from Latvia and Scandinavia. The first of these was a cargo of 213 standards brought by *Nordstjernen* for Megitt & Jones in August 1924. The same company also received a slightly larger cargo aboard *Antigoon* in June the following year. The other two consignments were for J D Lloyd & Co (whos yard is now the site of Gerddi Rheidol) and arrived aboard *Obero* in October 1924 and *Etne* in May 1926. Unloading the logs and deals took about a week. It was transported to the yards either by horse and cart in the case of Megitt & Jones or made into rafts and floated across the harbour to Trefechan where it would be cut into the sizes required. After these shipments all further consignments came by rail.

A three masted vessel, possibly *Obero* in the lower harbour, c 1924. Note the activity on St David's Quay.
(Photo Album 1263, PZ5464/12)

Branstone, owned by Burnham Shipping of Cardiff negotiates her way out of the harbour, c1923.
(Photo Album 1275, PZ5476/37)

Despite her sea-worn hull *Orenie* was only three years old when she visited Aberystwyth in May 1926 with a cargo of basic
slag and superphosphate for David Rees & Co.   (Photo Album 1262, PZ5463/25)

MV *Garthloch* paid numerous visits to Aberystwyth in 1927 carrying cargoes of roadstone. She was owned by Thomas Adams of St Dogmaels. Not an attractive vessel her rudimentary bridge arrangement indicates that she was crudely converted from a sailing vessel. (Photo Album 1262, PZ5463/7)

Two of the crew of *Overton* pause for a quick cigarette. *Matje* is alongside the quay behind her, November 1926. (Photo Album 1262, PZ5463/11)

Matje, once a familiar site along the North Wales coast when christened *Prince Jaja* unloads a mixed cargo of coal and bricks, November 1926.   (Photo Album 1262, PZ5463/3)

Monroe Bros *Dunvegan* arrives to collect a cargo of zinc and ore concentrates for Western Mining Co Ltd, October 1927.
(Photo Album 1262, PZ5463/2)

LOADING PZ 'PEGRIX' AT ABERYSTWYTH

Pegrix made one visit to Aberystwyth in July 1926 shortly after acquisition by Robert Rix & Sons of Hull. *Pegrix* was one of the very select band of steamers that came to load a cargo during the 1920s. She left with a cargo of over 200 tons of zinc ore concentrate obtained from reworking spoil tips at Frongoch Mines by the Cambrian Electrolytic Zinc Co.
(Photo Album 1263, PZ5464/5)

Pegrix makes her way to the harbour entrance, July 1926. Note the distinctive funnel markings and house flag The dilapidated state of the warehouse on St David's Quay is only too evident.   (Photo Album 1262, PZ5463/28)

Halton, owned by the "Overton Steamship Co Ltd" .   (Photo Album 1262, PZ5463/12)

The scenes on these two pages document both the visit of the largest vessel known to have visited Aberystwyth harbour as well as the last occasion in which three cargo carrying vessels were to be seen in the port at one time.

Mons of 631 grt and a length of 178 feet arrived from Swansea to load 400 tons of zinc ore and 60 tons of lead ore before departing for Antwerp. Both *Rockingham* and *Clareen* arrived with cargoes of coal for Capt W Griffiths, the former from Port Talbot, the latter from Cardiff. As described overleaf the arrival of *Rockingham* was blessed with greater fortune than that of *Clareen*. Registered at Dublin *Rockingham* was built in Wicklow in 1855 and had been employed in the coasting trade for seventy years. However having seen the fate that befell *Clareen* the crew of *Rockingham* deserted at Aberystwyth claiming that the vessel was unseaworthy.

Clareen is barely visible beneath the bows of *Mons*. *Rockingham* is in the foreground.   (Photo Album 1262, PZ5463/98)

Mons entering the harbour, March 1927. Note the rope from her bows to the capstan on the wooden jetty. (Photo Album 1275, PZ5476/62)

Mons at the quayside, 1927.

(Photo Album 1262, PZ5463/55)

Maralie entering the harbour.   *(Arthur Lewis Collection)*

Belfast registered *Glenshesk* visited Aberystwyth in June 1928 also with a cargo of bricks. (Photo Album 1262, PZ5463/6)

Maralie, owned by Service Navigation of Cardiff arrives to load a cargo of mineral concentrates. Her departure in May 1925 was less auspicious when she struck bottom going over the harbour bar. She also visited the town in 1928 with a cargo of bricks for Vaughan & Co who were then engaged in building houses at Penparcau. (Photo Album 1262, PZ5463/4)

Although the view of three cargo vessels in the harbour at one time in March 1927 was a welcome site to many in the town,

Capt O'Neill of the Waterford registered ketch *Clareen* was in no mood to enjoy the spectacle. His entry into the harbour was misjudged and as a result he collided with the stone jetty (see p.62). Some observers suggested that this was a result of the vessel having struck the bar on entry and being thrown off course. Whatever the cause, the result was that *Clareen*, built in Plymouth in 1884 and an irregular visitor to the port since 1902 was badly holed. She struggled up as far as the town quay where her cargo of coal for Capt

Griffiths was unloaded. Her fate then hung in the balance as her Irish owners decided whether she was worthy of repair or to be sold for breaking up. Sadly the latter option was exercised and *Clareen* broken up on the Trefechan side of the harbour near the malt kiln. Local children were often to be seen in the vicinity collecting the copper nails that fell into the mud. These were sold to a local scrap merchant, a jam jar full fetching sufficient to gain entry into one of the local cinemas.

Clareen seen in happier times, on her visit with a cargo of coal in August 1926 for Capt Griffiths' recently erected warehouse on St David's Quay. (Photo Album 1275, PZ5476/39)

Clareen about to collide with the stone jetty.

(Photo Album 1695, PZ6811/12)

Clareen being broken up on the Trefechan side of the harbour.

(Photo Album 1265, PZ5466/93)

Venus alongside the town quay. The empty berths on the quayside contrast markedly with today's crowded scene.
(Photo Album 706, PG221/100)

Weston was the last visitor from the "Overton Steamship Co Ltd", in March 1932.   (Photo Album 1262, PZ5463/5)

SS *Teifi* alongside St David's Quay c1927. (Photo Album 1262, PZ5463/26)

Enid Mary departing, c1934. (Photo Album 1262, PZ5463/42)

MV *West Coaster* heads into Cardigan Bay, 1938.　　　　　　　(Photo Album 1263, PZ5464/27)

These three photos all show vessels with a Cardigan connection. Seen alongside St Davids Quay c1927 is the grey- hulled *Teifi* owned by James Davies of Cardigan. *Teifi* paid a total of twelve visits to Aberystwyth between 1926 and 1930 before she sank in the Bristol Channel.

The other two vessels belonged to another Cardigan shipowner W G James who registered his company British Isles Coasters Ltd in 1934. *Enid Mary* visited the town both in 1934 and 1935. Being only a metre or so shorter than *Mons* (the longest vessel to use the harbour) she required careful and considered negotiation. In order to catch the tide her departure was timed for early morning, an atmosphere captured by photographer Arthur Lewis.

The third photograph shows the neat and pristine *West Coaster* on her maiden voyage in 1938. She made a total of nine visits bringing granite road chippings from Trefor, north Wales. On this her maiden voyage she was crewed by a predominantly Dutch crew. *West Coaster* was sold in 1943 and was later converted into a dredger. She was eventually broken up in 1984

The last steam powered vessel to bring a cargo into the harbour was Accomac, a 347 grt steamer built in Groningen in 1914. Previously known as *Dixley* and *Oakover* she was the property of Walford Lines Limited of London and discharged a part cargo of cement before departing to Cardigan with the rest of her cargo in August 1939.
(Photo Album 1275, PZ5476/54)

During the War Years the harbour saw only one visitor, the Manx steamer *Goldseeker*. This does not mean that the harbour was inactive. A guard was placed on the quay and only those with the requisite pass were able to proceed about their business. In addition two concrete pill boxes were built, one near the end of South Marine Terrace, the other, which still survives, on Penhuwcyn to guard the harbour entrance. Little fishing was carried on as most of those previously involved were on active service. Two RAF rescue launches were based in the harbour to search for downed aircrew, while David Williams the boat-builder continued to turn out a wide variety of craft including over 400 ships' lifeboats, 5 motor fishing vessels and over a hundred other boats of various descriptions.

The motor vessel *Venus* paid two trips to Aberystwyth in 1933 with cargoes of road chippings from Llanbedrog. She is seen here at low tide lying alongside the town quay.
(Photo Album 706, PG221/43)

THE
FISHING INDUSTRY

The inhabitants of Aberystwyth have been involved in fishing since time immemorial. References to herring fishing exist as far back as 1206, while many of the earliest views of the harbour show fishing boats or other fishing activity. The eighteenth century was one of particular importance as good catches of herring encouraged the building of fishing boats. Lewis Morris writing in 1748 called the town one of the greatest fisheries in Wales. He remarked on an incident that occured three years earlier when 47 fishing boats caught 1,111 barrelfuls of herring (around 1,360,800 fish) in one night. He was of the opinion that if there were a better harbour this would be a frequent event. During the herring season he noted that there was a glut of other fish including whiting, cod and pollack but little value was placed on these. He also noted the presence of bottle-nosed dolphins, porpoises, monkfish and blue sharks in the bay.

The herring season usually lasted from September to December. The usual method of fishing was for the boats to go out at sunset, shoot their nets and wait for an hour or so before bringing the first net in. If the catch was deemed ample then the other nets were hauled in and the boat sailed for home. As the boats used were quite small, the nets had to be emptied when the fishermen returned to land.

The decline in shipping using the harbour made more room available for fishing boats so that by 1872 there were eighty three fishing boats registered at Aberystwyth, though many of these belonged to New Quay, Aberaeron, Borth and Aberdyfi for which Aberystwyth was the port of registry. For administrative purposes fishing boats were divided into three categories. First class boats, of which there were two registered in 1872, were of 15 tons or over and navigable by means other than oars. Second class boats, of which there were six, were of less than 15 tons and also navigable by means other than oars. Third class vessels, to which the remainder belonged were navigable by oars only and usually used just for herring fishing and trips in the bay. The first class vessels were decked, had bunks and rudimentary accommodation and were usually manned by a crew of three. One of the favourite trawling grounds for these vessels was the gutter, a narrow depression with a clayey floor extending from five miles south west of Aberystwyth to New Quay Head. Catches were usually landed every other day. During the 1880s local fishmonger Francis Bennison was master of the steam trawler *Advance* which boasted a crew of six. He soon relinquished her in favour of the smaller *Albatross* as he said the expenses incurred with a steam trawler did not make it pay.

Another notable inhabitant who tried his hand at trawling was the artist Alfred Worthington who jointly purchased the *Eagle* with Captain Hughes, landlord of the Sailors Arms. He later purchased *Marcus Moxham* on his own account. Partly due to the reluctance of local fishermen to purchase boats of over twenty tons (which needed a passed master) and partly due to the richer and easier rewards to be had taking visitors on trips around the bay the fishing industry went into decline. Hotelier W H Palmer had also tried his hand at owning a fishing boat and aired his grievances, suggesting that the fishermen may also have been partly to blame. He claimed that anyone capable of commanding a vessel was too busy with holiday-makers to contemplate fishing, and locals would not sail with a captain from away. If they had a good haul the crew had no interest in going back to sea until that money was gone and adopted a cavalier approach to the maintenance of his nets. Consequently the initiative passed to fishermen from outside the area, most noticably from Hoylake who exploited the local fisheries with very little benefit to the local economy.

Among the second class vessels was a rig almost unique to Aberystwyth. This was a three masted boat usually about 7.5m in length and thought to have originated in Borth during the mid nineteenth century. The example shown, *Lizzie*, was a larger version and was used for trips in the bay during the summer months. To allow passengers on and off, the boats had to beach bows first, with the result that a wave hitting the stern would splash those inside. To counteract this a pointed stern, similar in shape to the bows, was developed during the late nineteenth century.

Many of the other second class boats were Morecambe Bay "nobbies" which were once common locally. They appear to have been used in Aberystwyth from the 1890s onwards for herring and mackerel fishing. They were usually half-decked with a central well and had a distinctive rounded stern. Their versatility ensured popularity for over half a century as they also made excellent pleasure boats. Even during the 1950s three were still to be seen in the harbour. The last of this class of vessel, the 35 ft *Suzie Wong* left in 1982 for renovation and display at the Industrial and Maritime Museum in Cardiff. *Suzie Wong* was built in Conwy during the 1930s and had been used as a pleasure boat since her arrival from Porthmadog in 1960.

Third class vessels also included a type of boat unique to the town, the *Aberystwyth Beach Boat*. These were made at the boatyard of David Williams & Sons in Queens Road and later at Trefechan. They evolved at the turn of the century from the double enders previously mentioned and operated on the same principle. These were used for trips in the bay and also fishing with drift nets. Usually about six metres long and two metres across they carried a crew of two when fishing. This was the type of boat favoured by Teddy James who operated the ferry across the harbour.

The disappearance of herring during the early years of the twentieth century to spawning grounds farther into the Irish

The sketch shows the type of vessel in use during the 1820s and probably little changed from fifty years before. Drift nets were used during the herring season, beam trawls at other times.

(Drawing Volume 317)

Fishing boats at Aberystwyth, c1840. Both sailing and rowing boats are shown. In the foreground are rays, dogfish and a pile of smaller fish, perhaps whiting.
(Welsh Primitive, Carmarthen Museum)

Sea had the anticipated effect. The distances involved (12 miles plus) were too great for the relatively fragile local boats so that by 1928 only ten boats were operating commercially. Of these only one was first class, *Crescent*, a trawler that fished nearly all year round between Aberystwyth and New Quay. Nine smaller boats were engaged in fishing for herring, whiting and mackerel. Three of these were rowing boats, the rest small motor vessels. It was estimated that 33 men derived employment from fishing, none full time.

Thirty years later some boats fished part time, mainly for mackerel, but tourists were still the most lucrative summer catch, with whiting and herring sought later in the year. Visits were made by *Willing Lad* from Milford Haven during the 1950s and a Scottish vessel *Boy Ken* in 1972, both dredging for scallops, but neither found it commercially viable.

Apart from lobster fishing, discussed elsewhere, many of the larger vessels in the harbour are now charter vessels used for taking groups of anglers on fishing trips, very often visiting wreck sites, of which many abound in Cardigan Bay.

Facing Page (Top).
Tan-y-bwlch beach c1837 showing a light erected to help the herring fishermen enter the harbour. The tramway led from Alltwen quarry to the stone pier, then being built.
(Welsh Primitive, Drawing volume 56)

Facing Page (Below).
Fishing smacks of the type used for fishing c1835.
(Welsh Primitive, Drawing volume 56)

Edith makes her way into the harbour in tranquil fashion, 1921.
(Photo Album 833, PZ8230/2)

A Morecambe Bay "nobby" and a double ended beach boat in the Gap, c1925.   (Photo Album 833, PZ4798/11)

Fishermen on the quay side, c1925 The 'nobby' *Snowdrop,* complete with fishing gear, is moored alongside the quay. The catch was usually divided into equal shares, one each for the crew and one each to pay for maintenance of the boat and nets.

(Photo Album 833, PZ4798/12)

The three masted boat *Lizzie* at work one summer c1900.
(Photo Album 1391, PZ5925/71)

The catch was either sold locally or salted and consigned in barrels by train to Milford Haven. Third from the right is Baden Davies, a popular local character and coxswain of the lifeboat.
(Photo Album 833, PZ4798/29)

Two fishing boats moored alongside the quay c1920. The smaller of the two is an Aberystwyth Beach Boat.
(Photo Album , PZ)

Fish was sold locally both by fishmongers such as the aforementioned Mr Bennison and by fish sellers, many of whom had their own regular pitch. Seen here with a fine selection of mackerel on her hand cart is Mrs Thomas, c1925. (Photo Album 1269, PZ5470/62)

Evan Daniel Jones selling mackerel on the quayside, c1930.
(Photo Album 1269 PZ5470/71)

LOBSTER FISHING

After 1945 further attempts were made to establish a lobster fishery. The availability of larger boats, many of them old ships' lifeboats and capable of carrying a larger number of pots proved invaluable. Previous attempts at lobster fishing had proved a failure as the loss of gear outweighed any catches made, but the site of French lobster boats off the coast of Wales convinced many that lobster fishing could be made to pay. By 1958 this was the dominant form of fishing with four vessels involved.

By the early 1980s an average of six tonnes of lobster were being landed at Aberystwyth annually. The Cardigan Bay lobster is regarded as being particularly tasty and the majority end up in fashionable restaurants in France. The most desirable size is 0.75 -1kg. It is said that lobsters off the coast of Aberystwyth are quite used to being handled as they have been caught and put back a number of times before being big enough to be taken.

A stroll along the quayside will show that two types of lobster pot predominate. Most popular are ink-well pots, usually made of galvanised wire or plastic. These are round with a flat top and base. The entrance is in the top while the base is weighted, usually with concrete. The second type is the creel. This has a flat rectangular base onto which arched struts are attached. Netting is then spread over the struts. The entrance is in the netting. Again the base is weighted with concrete. The pots are baited, usually with fish and left on the sea bottom in small clusters. A buoy is left on the surface to mark the spot. In the summer they will be checked daily. At the time of writing there are some half dozen boats wholly employed in lobster fishing as well as a number of part time fishermen.

Iles De Nord returning to harbour after checking her pots, the ever hopeful gulls in attendance.
(PG6165/2 Photo Album 2145)

Traditionally made creel type lobster pots on the quayside.
(Photo Album 2145, 199700014/1)

David Gestetner makes her way towards the harbour entrance and her next port of call . (Photo Album 2145, 199700014/3)

Sara M moored against the town quay and attracting a lot of admiration, 1987.   (Photo Album 2145, 199700014/3)

1945

TO THE PRESENT DAY -
OF MOTOR VESSELS AND MARINAS

After the Second World War the harbour saw a limited revival with visits by motor vessels such as *Dagny*, *Cranmere*, *Strijd* and *Eldorita* carrying cargoes of roadstone for Cardiganshire County Council. Visits by the last two vessels coincided in May 1950, the last occasion that two vessels were berthed in the harbour at the same time. On the Trefechan side of the harbour David Williams's boatyard continued to turn out a variety of well built and highly regarded boats, including *Ynys Enlli* and *Silver Wake*, two fishing boats that are still part of the harbour scene after more than thirty years.

Following the last visit by *Lady Sophia* in 1954, with a cargo of road chippings for the council, concerted efforts were made to secure further cargoes. Approaches were made to Shellmex, BP, Esso, Cementation and the Wholesale Coal Factors Association but all declined to use the harbour. It seemed that the future of the harbour now lay with a dwindling fishing fleet and increasingly with pleasure boats. In fact it would not be until 1972 that a vessel of any significance would grace the harbour. This was the *David Gestetner*, a converted Thames sailing barge with tan sails.

Chartered by the company whose name she bore, her visit was one of 47 scheduled stops in a little over ten weeks to publicise their reprographic products. Formerly called *Ethel*, she was built in Harwich in 1894.

As the emphasis changed and the harbour gradually and occasionally grudgingly came to be recognised as a leisure resource a yachting club was formed in the early 1950s and is still with us today, but now re-named the Aberystwyth Boating Club. Another aspect of pleasure boating in the form of TS Thunderer, used by the Sea Cadets, added animation to an otherwise empty looking harbour. A torrential downpour in September 1958 caused a flood that wrenched six boats from their moorings. A gale then blowing hastily consigned them to the deep. The 1960s saw the departure of the last of the pleasure boats offering trips in the bay, so long a feature of the town and still fondly remembered by many. The days when four or more of these boats would ply their trade from the beach opposite the bandstand have long gone. *Worcester Castle* was re-named *Skylark* and was last heard of in Tenby, whilst *Pride of the Midlands* was sold in 1966 to a London company for

sightseeing trips on the Thames, where she later sank after hitting a baulk of timber.

The unhurried but purposeful atmosphere that attends the pleasure and fishing boats in Aberystwyth harbour was rudely disturbed on October 23rd 1987 with the arrival of crowds of onlookers, including orange anoraked television crews, scanning the horizon for the arrival of the blue-hulled motor vessel *Sara M* with a cargo of 200 cubic metres of Swedish timber for Ystwyth Homes, a local building company. This was the first cargo to arrive by sea for thirty three years. *Sara M* was owned by the newly formed Ystwyth Shipping Limited, registered at Aberystwyth and crewed and captained by local men. Her master was Roger Meredith achieving his ambition of bringing a cargo into the harbour. Sadly this was to be her only visit to her home port as the following year she was sold.

The mud-flats shortly before work on the marina began in 1994.

(Photo Album 2145, 199700014/5)

Three boats of interest in the Gap c1980. *Suzie Wong* (centre left) is now in the Industrial & Maritime Museum, Cardiff. *Glasydorlan* was built at the nearby Lerry Boatyard, Borth and *Golden Wake* (extreme right) was owned locally for many years. All three have now left Aberystwyth.

(Photo album 2145, PG6165/4)

A Marina
for Aberystwyth ?

The first mention of a marina at Aberystwyth was as one of five options discussed by planning consultants Building Design Partnership in their Aberystwyth & District Plan published in 1972. This report recognised the harbour as a relatively undeveloped asset with regard to both local and tourist use. The marina envisaged in the report required dredging of the mud flats and building a new quay near St Davids Quay. This would give a permanent area of water for mooring and general boating use. Other recommendations included residential development on the town quay and acquisition and mooring of an old steam or sailing vessel to add character to the harbour. Recognised as being of more pressing importance was the need to rebuild the timber jetty, built in 1903 and now showing its age.

The idea lay dormant for another ten years until revived in a study by Mid Wales Development which saw the town as one of twelve major sailing centres around the Welsh coast. The plans envisaged first class marina facilities and associated developments. A further joint study with Ceredigion District Council produced a £7.2m scheme to include a harbour village with berths for 170 boats, flats, sheltered housing, a boat repair yard and a hotel. After a sometimes heated campaign, opposition from a number of groups and a degree of apathy on the part of the majority, Ceredigion District Council voted narrowly in favour of the proposed scheme in July 1983. Tenders were invited and initial response proved positive with nine different developers showing an interest. Public money totalling over £2m was made available from Mid Wales Development, Ceredigion District Council and the Welsh Development Agency. It seemed that a marina was on the way. Mid Wales Development also made grants available for schemes to increase facilities and tidy up both the Gap and the Town Quay. A subsequent government moratorium on public spending served to delay both these schemes and perhaps also to make a number of developers reconsider their position, especially as the estimated cost of the marina had mushroomed to an estimated £12m. Consequently when the closing date for proposals came and went in May 1986 only one proposal had been received. This scheme was deemed unsuitable as it went far beyond the original brief and included three times as many apartments as originally envisaged, up to 80 flats for use by UCW students which were not in the original guidelines and insufficient car parking. The reading

Fishing boats blockading the harbour in an anti-marina protest, 1993.
(Photo Album 1727, PG5843/3)

Diggers at work excavating the marina, 1994.

(Photo Album, 199600055/3)

of the Aberystwyth Harbour Act 1987 in the House of Commons in late 1986 now seemed superfluous. At least Mid Wales Development kept their promise and work on the Gap Improvement Scheme and the Town Quay Fishery Scheme commenced. Both were completed in April 1987 and cost a total of £616,000. Work on the Gap included provision of a retaining wall and a paved path where the Vale of Rheidol extension once ran. The Town Quay was strengthened in anticipation of dredging work (which now looked a remote possibility), and provision of better facilities for harbour users. The wisdom of the latter scheme seemed to be confirmed by a proposal from Captain Roger Meredith to use the Town Quay to export breeze blocks from Hendre Quarry to Ireland aboard a 450 ton Dutch Coaster *Joan T.*

For some years it seemed that to all intents and purposes the marina was dead and buried. But, in 1989 plans for a marina resurfaced. The proposal came from three local businessmen who envisaged a less ambitious scheme than proposed in 1983 with 105 berths, a hotel, flats and a chandlery. Public opposition was conducted with greater vigour than before and a petition of 2,500 names rapidly assembled. Once again Ceredigion District Council voted on the proposal and once again found in favour, having already demolished the old Sunday school in Trefechan in order to improve access to the site. The marina was to be a reality.

Dredging work commenced in Spring 1994 and continued throughout the summer. A barge was brought by tug from Liverpool to assist in the work. By the end of the exercise some 150,000 tons of mud had been removed and distributed either around the Marina or in the railway cutting behind Penyrangor. Pontoons were put in place, and despite teething troubles were soon in use. Phase I of the Marina was officially opened on September 22nd 1994 with the arrival of the round the world yacht *Maiden*.

As a result of the marina the harbour has enjoyed something of a rejuvenation with a variety of yachts and cabin cruisers giving a distinct air of prosperity. Visiting yachts, once uncommon enough to be objects of curiosity, are now an almost daily occurence during the summer months. The first ship since *Sara M* in 1987 made its way into the harbour in the face of a biting cold easterly wind in January 1996. This was a converted Norwegian whaler *Ocean Defender* now owned by environmental charity Earthkind. The visit was to draw attention to their work and as a precursor to their survey into dolphin numbers conducted later in the year in conjunction with Friends of Cardigan Bay. Since the old style lifeboats were superseded by inflatable craft in the 1960s the RNLI have based their lifeboat station in the harbour. Initially use was made of the storage sheds on the quayside but in 1994 a new purpose built boat shed was built to house a new larger Atlantic 21 class Inshore Lifeboat.

Aberystwyth's RNLI Inshore Lifeboat, 1994.
(Photo Album 2145, 199700014/2)

The barge used in further excavations, 1994.

(Photo Album 2145, 199600055/4)

An affluent flotilla moored at the marina.

(Photo Album 2145,199600055/1)

...other view of the marina, 1996.

(Photo Album 2145, 199600055/2)

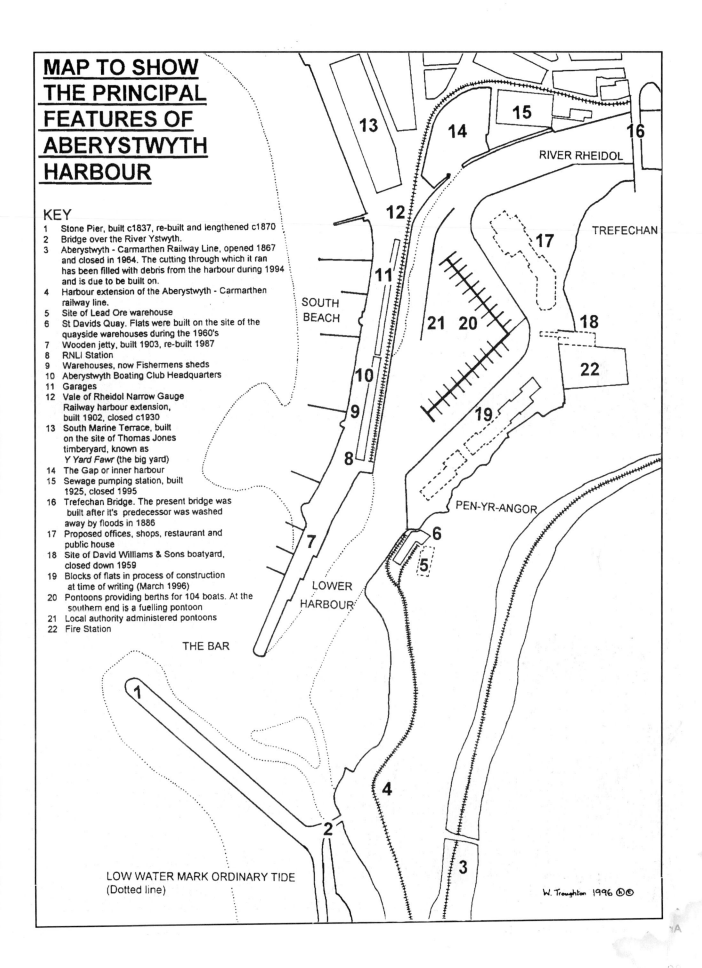

MAP TO SHOW THE PRINCIPAL FEATURES OF ABERYSTWYTH HARBOUR

KEY

1. Stone Pier, built c1837, re-built and lengthened c1870
2. Bridge over the River Ystwyth.
3. Aberystwyth - Carmarthen Railway Line, opened 1867 and closed in 1964. The cutting through which it ran has been filled with debris from the harbour during 1994 and is due to be built on.
4. Harbour extension of the Aberystwyth - Carmarthen railway line.
5. Site of Lead Ore warehouse
6. St Davids Quay. Flats were built on the site of the quayside warehouses during the 1960's
7. Wooden jetty, built 1903, re-built 1987
8. RNLI Station
9. Warehouses, now Fishermens sheds
10. Aberystwyth Boating Club Headquarters
11. Garages
12. Vale of Rheidol Narrow Gauge Railway harbour extension, built 1902, closed c1930
13. South Marine Terrace, built on the site of Thomas Jones timberyard, known as *Y Yard Fawr* (the big yard)
14. The Gap or inner harbour
15. Sewage pumping station, built 1925, closed 1995
16. Trefechan Bridge. The present bridge was built after it's predecessor was washed away by floods in 1886
17. Proposed offices, shops, restaurant and public house
18. Site of David Williams & Sons boatyard, closed down 1959
19. Blocks of flats in process of construction at time of writing (March 1996)
20. Pontoons providing berths for 104 boats. At the southern end is a fuelling pontoon
21. Local authority administered pontoons
22. Fire Station

RIVER RHEIDOL

TREFECHAN

SOUTH BEACH

PEN-YR-ANGOR

LOWER HARBOUR

THE BAR

LOW WATER MARK ORDINARY TIDE
(Dotted line)

W. Troughton 1996 ℗©

Ocean Defender manouevering in the lower harbour shortly after arrival, January 1996. (Photo Album 2145,19970038/1)

The quayside showing the new RNLI boatshed opened in 1994.   (Photo Album 2145, 199700038/2)

ABERYSTWYTH HARBOURMASTERS

Capt D J Lloyd

Aberystwyth Harbourmasters badge presented to the trustees by Matthew Davies, Cwmcynfelin. Dated 1789 it is now in the Ceredigion Museum.

Lt. Cdr. P Norrington-Davies

Richard Morgan, *1770 to 1780.*

John Griffith, *1780 to 1781.* Relieved of his duty for not having relieved vessels entering the harbour of theirs.

William Jobson, *1781 to 1782.* Neglected the duty of his office and absconded.

Lewis Evans, *1782 to 1785.* Resigned.

Edward Humphreys, *1788 to 1806.*

Lewis Evans, *1806 to 1808.*

John Lewis, *1808 to 1819.* Resigned.

Captain William Williams, *1819 to 1823.* Once master of the ship *Lively*, died in office.

Captain John Davies, *1823 to 1836.* Died in office.

Captain Thomas Jones, *1837 to 1841.* Lived in the Nelson Inn on Marine Terrace. Was reputed to have worn silver buckles on his shoes.

Richard Page, *1842 to 1850.* A civil engineer, he may have been involved with improvements then being made at the harbour.

Captain John Jones, *1850 to 1863.* Master of *John and Anne,* a locally built 46 ton sloop.

Captain John Davies, *1863 to 1874,* master of *Magdalene*, a 114 ton schooner built in Aberystwyth in 1841. Died in office.

Edward Jones, *1876 to 1881.* Dismissed for neglecting his duties.

Captain John Thomas, *1881 to 1901.* First appointed at a salary of £70 a year.

Captain Henry Humphreys *1901 to 1909.* His first taste of the sea was as a boy with his father who was master of the schooner *Capricorn*. Died in office aged 64.

Captain D J Lloyd *1909 to 1926.* Went to sea at the age of twelve. Went on to command numerous vessels including the barque *Hope* and the steamer *Isle of Anglesey.*

Captain David Jones *1926 to 1929.* First went to sea on his fathers boat *Zouave* when aged 13 years old. Resigned his post to go back to sea.

Captain William James *1929.* Retired on grounds of ill health. Lived at Caledfryn, Bryn Road.

Captain Griffith Roberts *1929-1932.* Had experience in both merchant and royal navies.

Captain David Jones *1932-1948.* Resumed his former position after three years at sea. Resided at Iolanthe, Lisburne Terrace.

Capt H Julian Jones *1948 to1952.* Had worked for both P&O and Cunard before being invalided out of the merchant navy in 1944. Presided over a brief revival in the fortunes of the harbour

Captain G E Roberts OBE *1953 to 1961.* Previously worked for Lamport & Holt. Was awarded the OBE for his wartime service.

Captain H Julian Jones *1961 to 1968.*

Capt Herber Evans *1968 to 1980.* Before taking up the post of harbourmaster captained BP tankers including the 100,000 ton *British Admiral.*

Captain Jack Williams *1980 to 1994.* Had been in the merchant navy for 42 years before being appointed harbourmaster. Was employed by Port Line and had commanded some of the worlds largest refrigerated cargo ships including the 23,000 ton *Port Caroline.*

Lieutenant Commander Peter Norrington-Davies *1994 to present day.* A popular charter boat operator with seventeen years Royal Navy experience, mainly in submarines. Commanded HMS Walrus 1982-1986 prior to leaving the Royal Navy in 1989.

BIBLIOGRAPHY, FURTHER READING & ACKNOWLEDGEMENTS

Aberystwyth Shipping Records, NLW Dept of Manuscripts & Records.

R S Fenton, *Cambrian Coasters* (Kendal, 1989).

David Jenkins, *Cardiff Shipowners* (Cardiff, 1986).

J Geraint Jenkins, *The Inshore Fishermen of Wales* (Cardiff, 1991).

E J Jones, *Economic History of Wales* (London, 1928).

W J Lewis, *Born on a Perilous Rock* (Aberystwyth, 1980).

R J H Lloyd, 'Aberystwyth Fishing Boats', *Mariners Mirror*, 41 (1955), 149-161.

Marwolaeth Cadben Evan Hughes, *Yr Eurgrawn Weslyaidd*, XI, no7 (1848), 218.

T H Merchant, "Aberystwyth Harbour since 1925", *Ceredigion*, Vol IV no 3 (1962), 283-289.

T H Merchant, 'New Life For Aberystwyth Harbour', *Sea Breezes* vol xlvi, (1972),.

T H Merchant, 'Aberystwyth's Harbour Trade', *Ships Monthly*, Vol 19, no. 2 (February 1984), 34-35.

Gerald Morgan, 'The Aberystwyth Brig *Renown* 1816-1841', *NLW Journal,* XXVIII, No.3 (1994), 291-298.

Gerald Morgan, 'North Cardiganshire Shipbuilding, 1700-1880', Occasional Papers in Ceredigion History, Number 2 (Aberystwyth, 1992).

J Morgan (late J Cox), *New Guide to Aberystwyth* (Aberystwyth, 1874).

Lewis Morris, *Plans in St George's Channel -1748* (Beaumaris, 1987).

A C Simpson, *The Lobster Fishery of Wales* (London, 1956).

W Troughton, 'The Barque *Hope* of Aberystwyth', *Ceredigion*, Vol XII, no3 (1995), 85-100.

Basil Underhill, *Deep Water Sail* (Glasgow, 1952).

I should like to thank the following for their assistance in the preparation of this book; the staff of the printing and photographic sections of the National Library of Wales, Mr Des Davies, Mr Patrick Mc Kenna of Drogheda, Dr D H Owen, Mr Iwan M Jones, Dr Paul Joyner, Mr T H Merchant, Mr R Iestyn Hughes, Mr Lyn L Davies, Mr David Jenkins, Lt. Cdr. P. Norrington-Davies.